The Storm of Our l

The Storm of Our Lives

*A Vietnamese Family's Boat
Journey to Freedom*

TAI VAN NGUYEN

McFarland & Company, Inc., Publishers
Jefferson, North Carolina, and London

FRONTISPIECE: The boat in 1983 by a local photographer standing on the riverbank in Phuoc Ly, Vietnam. It was used to obtain traveling permits from the Vietnamese government. All photographs are from the author's collection.

LIBRARY OF CONGRESS CATALOGUING-IN-PUBLICATION DATA

Nguyen, Tai Van, 1969–
  The storm of our lives : a Vietnamese family's boat journey to freedom / Tai Van Nguyen.
      p.   cm.
  Includes index.

  ISBN 978-0-7864-4176-1
  softcover : 50# alkaline paper ∞

  1. Nguyen, Tai Van, 1969– 2. Vietnamese American women — Biography. 3. Vietnamese Americans — Biography. 4. Boat people — Vietnam — Biography. 5. Political refugees — Vietnam — Biography. 6. Political refugees — United States — Biography. I. Title.
  E184.V53N486 2009
  973'.04959220922 — dc22   2009019472
  [B]

British Library cataloguing data are available

On the cover: The five surviving siblings, from left: Tu, Hue, Tai (the author), Ly, and Tuan in front of a Catholic church in Galang Refugee Camp, Indonesia, in 1984. Background ©2009 Shutterstock.

Manufactured in the United States of America

McFarland & Company, Inc., Publishers
  Box 611, Jefferson, North Carolina 28640
  www.mcfarlandpub.com

To my father,
who delivered us to the
lands of the free

Acknowledgments

    I would like to thank my former college professor, our family friend Chris Merlier, and my good friends Joan Herman, and Suzan Ruhe, for reading and correcting this manuscript. I would like to thank my father-in-law, Hoa Nguyen, and my beloved mother for their contributions on priceless cultural, historical, and familial background. I would like to thank Angelo Stalis of my local ABC television station for his weather information. I would like to thank all my coworkers, clients, former teachers, and friends for their gifts of knowledge and invaluable inputs to the story.

    I would like to thank all my relatives, especially my grandparents, uncles, and aunts — some of whom are still struggling in Vietnam — for their financial help in putting our boat together and for their prayers for us to have a safe journey. I would like to thank each and every one we met in Indonesia, all had a profound effect on our survival in Galang Refugee Camp. These included many wonderful Indonesians, Vietnamese "boat people," and foreigners who worked for organizations like the United Nations High Commission for Refugees, to help us resettle in the United States. I would like to thank my uncle, Dr. Robert Nguyen, and his wife, Ruth, for their sponsoring us to come to America. They spent so much time, energy, and money on us at the beginning so our family could have an easier transition into American society. I would like to thank my brothers Tuan and Tu and my sisters Ly and Hue for their painful recollection of our tragic events. In addition, I thank them for their wisdom, courage, resilience, and faith in God that saved all of us from the raging sea. Without these angels' helping hands, I would not be living in America and writing this book.

I would like to thank my beautiful wife, Kimberly, who has given me two wonderful children, Tyla and Tyvan. These children are my joy and comfort. They are the catalyst and the inspiration that have triggered my motivation to write this book. They give me the warmth and the love of a family that has seemingly existed for generations.

Lastly, I would like to thank my beloved father to whom this book is dedicated. Even though his life was short, out of love he did so much for us. He brought me into this world and taught me about Christ. He took us away from the Communist regime and delivered us to the lands of the free. Because of him, we were granted a special asylum to live in the greatest country in the world. By watching him and learning from him, I have become the kind of father that he once was.

Thank you all from the bottom of my heart.

Contents

Preface

After the fall of the U.S.–backed South Vietnamese government to the North Vietnamese Communists in April 1975, many Vietnamese people faced political and religious persecution from the new government. Constantly dealing with economic hardship and the lack of personal freedom, many of these people had no other choice but to get out of Vietnam. More than 840,000 Vietnamese asylum seekers left the Communist regime and arrived in the countries of Southeast Asia and Hong Kong. These people, who came to be known as the "boat people" risked their lives at sea in search for freedom.

Thousands of these people left loved ones behind and set out on the unpredictable water, and were tragically never heard from again. The raging South China Sea swallowed these people alive and left them no stories to tell. But many lived to tell of their terrible ordeals. I was one of the survivors who could give a complete account of what might have gone wrong during these journeys for freedom. The horrific tales of the ones who did not make it to safe shores remain untold at the bottom of the deep sea. Our family's escape was fraught with tragedy and danger from start to finish, and we would not have become living testimony without the sacrifice of our beloved father and the grace of the merciful God.

I never had the urge to write about my family's tragic journey until one day when I was watching my two small children playing with their toys in front of me. My heart moved when they ran over and gave me a surprising hug. Their actions were naturally innocent and yet so powerful that old memories came back into my mind. My vision became uncontrolably blurry. For a moment I thought I was my father and that my kids were me. Our love for each other was so enormous that nothing on earth could have explained it. At this very moment, the thought of my father reignited the fire inside me that had been extinguished for a long time. This fire immediately brought me the desire and the inspiration to begin the writing of this book.

Writing my family's story allowed me an opportunity to praise and thank the living God. It provided me with peace of mind and closure to an unforgettable family tragedy. And, it gave me a chance to pass on to my children and their children some cultural perspective, historical facts, and a bridge between my father and them, so that future generations might know why, where, when, and how their ancestors immigrated, so that the roots of our family would never be forgotten.

DAY 1

The Storm of Our Lives

"*Ba!*" screamed Tuan, my oldest brother, while at the helm navigating our boat, in response to a thud that brought the running engine to a complete halt. Tuan's intense scream clearly indicated that something seriously wrong had happened to our father in the boat's engine room. His cry jolted me awake instantly. I quickly sat up and looked back into the engine cabin where I saw our father, who appeared to be stooping over the boat's transmission behind the stalled motor. Immediately, I crawled toward our father but Tuan and my other older brother, Tu, who had been on the back outboard a moment before, beat me to our father's location. Inside the low profile of our boat compartment, it only took me about four paces on my hands and knees but I felt like I was running, out of breath, once I got to him.

Our father was in a very unusual position. The lower half of his body was still lying on the wooden boards that covered the whole engine room; the upper half disappeared into the opening to the engine where two wooden boards had been removed to expose the engine and the transmission. His head was down low enough that his short black hair was touching the bilge water. A small abrasion was clearly visible near his right temple; his eyes were tightly closed. His right arm, hanging over the transmission, appeared to be broken at the elbow; and his whole body embraced the engine and the transmission tightly as if he was hugging them. The bottom part of his gray jacket was wound tightly around the steel propeller shaft that connected the engine to a separate transmission. Our father was stuck, and badly hurt, as my first observation indicated. He neither moved nor spoke, but I still saw his

3

trim stomach inflating and deflating at a slow, steady pace. Some foam was slowly bubbling out of his mouth and nose while he faintly exhaled.

Tuan and Tu tried to take off my father's jacket to set him free, but the garment had twisted very tight; my brothers nervously kept yanking and pulling on it to no avail. I crawled on my hands and knees in the scant space around our father to offer some assistance, but I could not help at all. "*Ba! Ba! Ba sao roi?*" I screamed, asking if he was okay while vigorously shaking his back. He did not answer. Within a second, my eyes were flooded with tears and everything in front of me became blurry. I sensed doom. In the small, confined space, I screamed louder and louder, urging our father to respond. My two sisters were crying their lungs out in the adjacent front compartment where the three of us had been resting. With all the commotion going on, Tu, with the hottest temper in the family, became frustrated and yelled at us, "*Im het! Tai, di ra ngoai!*" ("Everbody shut up! Tai, go outside!") I obliged and crawled through a small square door to the back outboard, the helm area, leaving my two brothers tending our hurting father with a little more space and breathing room in the engine compartment.

Unable to pull the jacket off our father, Tu now had a long knife in his right hand and tried to cut away the jacket to free him. The knife had a decently sharp blade that we used for filleting fish. Our father's high-quality homemade jacket, lined with fabric from an old military parachute, had rolled up and twisted — by the winding action of the propeller shaft — into a wrist-sized nylon rope. With the sharpest knife onboard, my brother — breathing heavily like a coal miner and sweating like a marathon runner worked at the jacket as if he was cutting a metal pipe with a dull hacksaw. Tuan patted our father's back and yelled repeatedly "*Ba sao roi?*" There was neither verbal nor physical response from our father.

Our father was a river fisherman in a small village named Phuoc Ly, located about twenty miles from Ho Chi Minh City, formerly called Saigon, Vietnam. The village probably had about two thousand residents, and it was the biggest town within a three-mile radius, where large rivers and farmlands served as boundaries. A majority of the population worked and earned their living as farmers and fishers. Some operated small retail businesses; a few manufactured foods and goods; others offered skilled services; and the rest went to larger towns for jobs. Being in a small town, we had just one of everything. We had one Catholic church, one Buddhist temple, one school, one market, one bridge, and one main road that connected us to other villages. All other smaller roads led to dead ends.

From my village, I could go to Ho Chi Minh City, the largest city in the south part of the country by using my bicycle — our most common mode of transportation. It would take me about four hours to get to the city. It did not take that long for me to paddle. People had to wait for the ferries at the two large rivers, Cat Lai and Thu Thiem, inconveniently prolonging the trip. The government operated large ferries at these two rivers, but they only started up their ferries a couple times a day. All river crossers had to pay for the ferry fare at the gates, and then they had to pay again to have private citizens with smaller boats to transport them across the rivers. This situation had created many mishaps as occasionally small, overloaded boats went under, costing human lives and properties.

I call our father a fisherman because our family owned a fishing boat, but we did not make a living from fishing. Our family had actually been in the business of making tofu for quite some time. We were the only tofu makers in town. We made and sold it fresh daily at the market to the public. Not only did people like it fresh, they had to buy and eat it fresh because nobody had any refrigerators to keep food from spoilage. In fact, we did not even have electricity. Tofu sitting in a warm tropical temperature would certainly turn into bean curds overnight. Whenever we had a bad day at the market, our whole family would have nothing but tofu for supper. It seemed cool at first — people always praised tofu for its nutritional values, for being high in protein, comparable to meat without the bad fat — but when one ate it almost everyday, it was a different story. I used to whine to our mother about eating tofu; she simply gave me two choices: eating it or not eating at all. In order to stay alive, I did the right thing by stuffing it down my throat.

Besides being a fisherman, our father was also a farmer during the wet months. The tropics had two seasons: one wet and one dry. There was no freshwater irrigation system available for farming; therefore, our farming was strictly dependent on Mother Nature. Because the aridity of the soil prevented the development of good crops, only the popular, hardy yams and cassava could be grown. Both crops could be eaten in place of rice when rice was not available. In addition to that, cassava could be used to make tapioca, which our family made some-times — another way we made a living. The mostly clay field had been left fallow for years before our father acquired it for cultivation. He worked very hard to make it fruitful. He had read some books about agriculture that recommended the planting of sesame seeds and peanuts in order to put extra nutrients back into the soil once every few years. Therefore, every year he used a fourth or a fifth of his farm acreage to plant these supposedly beneficial crops, which were so unprofitable to us because they did not give high yields in the type of soil we had. After the harvest, our father put all the green plants in a huge hole in the dirt to make organic compost for the following seasons. We consumed most of our produce and we would sell the excess to our neighbors at a very cheap price.

The author's father in a military uniform, around 1972 in Le Van Duyet Camp, Saigon, Vietnam.

This farming business saved our family from starvation in the years of 1980 and 1981 when some rice-producing regions in Vietnam were nearly wiped out, due partly to human intervention and partly to Mother Nature. The government tried to build hydroelectric dams along the rivers, supposedly to provide fresh water to the crops. Without regular fresh water during growing seasons, some rice growers suffered disastrously. Meanwhile, the southernmost area of the heavily rice-growing region of the country was bombarded with frequent floods, which doubled the economic trouble of rice production. In addition to that, the government was exporting rice to some countries to pay off their debts owed during the Vietnam War, which quadrupled the crisis to rice consumers.

However, the thing that inflicted the most damaging effects was the governmental management and distribution of foods by allotment. The government controlled the movement of rice within different communities. Individuals were banned from transporting it commercially across town, which in turn made it readily available in one region and very scarce in another. The socialist government was supposed to collect rice from different regions and then to distribute it equally among its citizens throughout the country. Unfortunately, their plans were not working the way they envisioned. In certain parts of the country, people had plenty of rice to eat; and in some other parts like where we lived, people could not even find a grain.

The laws about the movement of foods did not apply just to rice; they affected other kinds of foods, as well as fuel and medicine. For instance, our family used soybeans to make tofu, but where we lived the soil was not compatible for growing the beans. We had to buy them from so-called "illegal smugglers" who transported the beans from the growing regions to different areas of the country to make a little profit. These transporting vendors were subject to arrest and seizure. Occasionally, the government tightened up their security, making lives of those "smugglers" more difficult, which in turn caused the price of the "illegal" goods to skyrocket. The consumers then had to pay extra for the final products. In effect, all businesses slowed down as the result of high prices. Sometimes, our family could not find soybeans to buy or they were too expensive to purchase, and we had to do something else to make a living in the meantime.

Before and during those difficult years, our father had sliced up and sun-dried all our produced yams and cassava, and stored them in boxes stacked underneath our beds. For almost two whole years, rice as a scarce commodity was so expensive that our family ate only dried yams and cassava to survive. We ate them so much and for so long that a lot of us, mostly young children, started to develop skin rashes and pimples. The more we filled our stomachs with yams and cassava, the more unhealthy symptoms showed up. There was no cure; unless we started eating rice again, they would not go away. Unfortunately, we did not have other alternatives to choose from. It was so hard, but at least we were fortunate people who had something to eat. Many less fortunate people depended on wild vegetables, garden snails, crickets, grasshoppers, snakes, lizards, frogs, field mice, and other crawling creatures to survive. And those poor critters even became hard to find after a while.

Thanh, eleven years of age, one of my good classmates, lived among the rice fields. One time I hung out with him at his place. There was nothing to do; therefore, he asked me to go hunting for field rats with him. I agreed. The two of us, along with his four-legged canine friend, got onto his family's ten-foot fishing boat and rowed to a remote location where there was thick vegetation on both banks of the river. Thanh handed me a homemade spear, grabbed another one, and jumped into the shallow water of the riverbank. Already ahead of him, his hunting partner was barking at some rushes. They were yelling, hollering, and beating up the surrounding vegetation as if there were more than two of them doing the work. I felt out of place by sitting on the boat alone, so I jumped into the water to join them with the weapon in my right hand. Before I realized how cold the water was, a rat as big as a raccoon flew out of a bush and hit my chest. At that moment, I believed my heart left my body for a few ticks of the clock. I crumpled and submerged my whole body in the water. Thanh barked out an order to me to go after the creature with my spear. Soaking wet, I stood straight up and poked repeatedly at the gray-furred animal that was getting away from me. The rodent was not swimming; he was actually *running* on the water surface, as fast as a water jet. Lucky for him, this was the first time in my life using a spear; he lived to see another day.

We spent the next three or four hours tearing up the banks of the river. It must have been a good day for those rats, because many of them escaped my killer blade. As a matter of fact, I could not hit any of them with my newly acquired weapon. However, I did learn a lot and had a lot of fun in the mud. Thanh and his hunting friend managed to take four lives. Having enough for supper, he then stopped for the day. On the riverbank, he placed all his catch in a small pile of dry hay and started the hay burning with a match. After a few minutes, what was left were some black ashes and four charred critters. Thanh skillfully used his spear blade to separate the heads, limbs, and tails. He then dexterously skinned the animals and cleaned out their guts, using the river water, to yield four pieces of white meat. They looked good. We got back onto the boat and headed home. Thanh offered me half of his catch. However, I had to gratefully refuse his generosity, because I knew our family did not and could not consume anything out of the norm, which only included beef, pork, chicken, duck, and seafood.

Similarly, our cautious family would not eat any vegetable whose source was unknown. One time, while turning dirt to look for fighting crickets in a fallow field, I came upon a wild mushroom bigger than a large Pizza Hut pizza. While happily hopping home to surprise our parents with our vegetable for the day, a middle-aged man stopped me and offered to buy it from me. I was thinking to myself, "He wants it; this must be some kind of special stuff that I did not know about; I have to show it to our parents." I quickly answered, "*khong*" ("no"), and I sprinted home, while feeling very good about myself. As soon as our father saw the mushroom, he demanded that I should toss it into the trash and go wash my hands immediately, since many had died from eating poisonous ones.

We had a cat named Miu that had the responsibility of controlling our rodent problems at home. Sadly, Miu was as skinny as we were, due to the decline of the rodent population. In addition to that, we did not have enough food to eat at home; therefore, there was not enough leftover food provided for him, so he wandered to neighbors' homes and preyed on their young chickens. Angry neighbors raised their voices and demanded answers. Our parents had no choice but to give him away to an extremely poor neighbor's family across the street. We all knew exactly what those hungry people were going to do to our pet. My two sisters and I were mad at our culpable parents for days, but we the children finally understood the situation. Our parents did what they had to do to keep everybody at peace.

In addition, at this time, somehow, some fish in the rivers developed some kinds of skin diseases that produced pus and rashes all over their skin. These fish looked so disgusting that no sane people wanted to eat them; if we did not even know if they were safe to eat or we were dared to try when all of us were so hungry and tempted. The government did recommend that people not consume these "sick" fish and they opportunistically blamed it on leached Agent Orange, which the "evil Americans" had used against the Communists during the war.

Between 1962 and 1971, the U.S. armed forces had sprayed seventy-seven million liters of this herbicide in South Vietnam as part of a defoliant program to deny cover for the Vietnamese Communists. As law-abiding citizens, most people just accepted this for what it was said to be. Of course, there were also some rumors going around that the government had released some types of by-product toxins into the water, which caused the fish to deform. However, anybody caught spreading such rumors criticizing their own government would do time. After a couple of local people went to jail because of saying those "stupid" things, the rest got intimidated. Then rumors died down in a hurry.

Even though we lived in the tropics and many rivers surrounded us, clean, fresh water was a scarce commodity during the dry seasons. Without rainwater, river water became brackish. Most water coming from shallow wells could not be used for drinking and cooking because it contained so much contamination from leached minerals and human pathogens. Only a few extremely deep, concrete-enforced wells in the village had clean groundwater which the owners would sell by the buckets. Our family was one of those that had to buy water that way daily during the dry spells.

During the wet months, we collected rainwater from our house rain gutters and stored it in large ceramic containers and metal drums for later use. There was plenty of rainwater during the wet seasons, as some rainstorms would last several weeks. In our backyard, next to our shallow well, our father had built a large brick and cement cistern that could hold the heavenly water during those wet months. This precious water would last us two or three months into the dry season. This was only for drinking and cooking. Water for other utilities, such as washing and bathing, came from our shallow well.

Besides being a fisherman and a farmer, our father was also a locksmith, tailor, small grocery owner, and so on. Most of the time, he augmented our family income by holding down two or three jobs at a time. I have been told that he was a multifarious individual, doing hundreds of jobs; whatever would feed his entire family. However, the job our father held that most affected my life and my family's life was the one where he served in the South Vietnamese government during the Vietnam War. He was a sergeant working in a military supply division stationed near Le Van Duyet Camp in Saigon, a camp that housed military families. My brothers, sisters, and I all grew up in that military camp.

Occasionally, our father flew out with a crew to test-jump some parachutes that his group repaired or tailored and packed. His main duty was manufacturing and packing military parachutes. He served for more than a decade in the military, but there was only one time when he had to be near the crossfire of battle. In 1972, his unit was deployed to Cambodia for two weeks to deliver military supplies to troops at the battlefront. At home, our mother became ill, but she maintained her prayers day and night. My father returned safe and sound.

Besides serving in the military, our father also volunteered, working as a leader of a group of boys — similar to the Boy Scouts of America — who were living in our military camp. His group taught soldiers' young sons basic survival skills and provided them with activities such as camping and traveling while most of their parents were away on duty. Our mother was strictly staying home, raising her children, and our father steadily held that military job to feed his eight-member family through thick and thin. At the end of the Vietnam War, our father lost his job. Our lives were upside down. We moved out of Saigon to Phuoc Ly, located about three miles from Bac Minh, where our grandparents lived.

Vietnam is an independent Southeast Asian nation located on the Indochinese peninsula. The Socialist Republic of Vietnam is bordered by China to the north, Laos to the northwest, and Cambodia to the southwest. The long stretch of S-shaped Vietnam's east coast fronts the South China Sea. With more than eighty-five million people, Vietnam is the thirteenth most populous country in the world. Most of the northern part of the country is a thick, mountainous jungle. In the heavily populated and cultivated Red River delta, rice is the main crop. The climate is monsoonal with frequent floods. A flat, marshy, muddy coast — the Mekong River system, dominates the southern part. The year-round tropical climate and rich soil yield abundant rice harvests. The people's heritage of more than one thousand of years of vassalage to the Chinese exists in language, art, and customs — the Confucian ethic. While scientific socialism is the official creed, the Buddhist faith is fairly well tolerated, because up to 85 percent of the population identify with Buddhism even though they do not practice on a regular basis. Our family is part of the approximately 8 percent of the people who are Roman Catholic.

Originally, the Vietnamese lived in China's Yellow River valley but they were driven south and then inhabited the Red River delta. They were under Chinese rule from around the 2nd century B.C. to the 900s, when they revolted and founded their own empire. They remained independent until the mid–nineteenth century when the French took control of Indochina. A western-style system of modern education was developed throughout the country. At the same time, Christianity was introduced into Vietnamese society. While developing a plantation economy to promote the exports of tobacco, rubber, indigo, coffee, and tea, the French deliberately ignored increasing calls for self-government and civil rights. During World War II, Japan occupied all of Vietnam. In 1945, when the war was over, the China- and Soviet-backed Viet Minh, a Communist and nationalist liberation movement, revolted in Hanoi and proclaimed the Democratic Republic of Vietnam. Ho Chi Minh led the Communists in an eight-year guerrilla war against the French, who were defeated in 1954 at Dien Bien Phu, North Vietnam, which allowed Ho to negotiate a ceasefire with a favorable position at the ongoing Geneva conference of 1954. According to the Geneva Agreements, the country was divided at the seventeenth parallel into two countries: Ho Chi Minh's Communist North Vietnam and Ngo Dinh Diem's nationalist South after the example of Korea. This was supposed to be temporary, pending an election in 1954 which never took place.

Before the border was sealed, there were three days during which citizens of both sides could travel freely across the border without any restrictions. Being Catholic residents of the North, both our wise grandparents' families and many villagers thought that the South would offer more religious freedom and economic opportunity, so they all decided to migrate to the South. At the time, our father, seventeen years of age, and our mother, fifteen — living in the village called Tien Nha — knew each other but they were not yet married. They, along with their families and many other villagers were picked up and transported by old French military trucks to Hai Phong Harbor. For a whole, long night, they all sat restlessly in the overcrowded bed of a truck with very little personal belongings, to get to the harbor. Small boats took them out to a large cruise ship that carried them — along with thousands of other refugees onboard — on a three-day, three-night exodus to the South. They were dropped off at the Bach Dang Harbor of Thu Thiem River, in Saigon.

Our father's family was not that wealthy but they did own some gold when they fled from the North. Life would have become easier for them if a place of residence could have been secured. They met a nice local man who was willing to help them buy his house in Thu Thiem. As it turned out, the man was not so nice after all; he was actually deceitful. The house was not even his. He took all my grandparents' gold and disappeared without a trace.

Now, as poor refugees, with no home and no money, like everybody else, they had no choice but to move to a designated area to settle under the government's direction. This new land was nothing but jungles filled with wild brush and trees. The new government of the South used tractors to clear the vegetation for roads and farmland, and provided food, hand tools, and crop seeds to all settlers so they could start their new lives. Our grandparents' families built their own homes from scratch and grew their own foods on the land. The two families had multiplied to a few hundred people by the time I came into existence.

World War II was the turning point in the history of Vietnam. From it emerged the Cold War, involving mainly the Soviet Union and the United States, which started over the control of Germany. In 1949, the Soviet Union had their first atomic bomb developed, which posed a threat to the United States and forced U.S. president Harry Truman to accept Britain's hegemony offer. Immediately, the United States acted, forming the Truman Doctrine to protect the "right of all people" around the world. The Truman Doctrine led to U.S. involvement in many international conflicts, which included Vietnam as a response to the Soviets' political expansion in Asia.

Ngo Dinh Diem, prime minister of the Democratic Republic of Vietnam in the South, faced a ruined economy, refugee problems, and religious and political turmoil. The Communists of the North established agrarian reform, rebuilt industries, and embarked on a campaign to overthrow the South. In 1961, the United States sent military advisors to the South and the U.S. role gradually escalated. The South Vietnamese government, backed by the United States, was unable to defeat the insurgent guerrillas, the Viet Cong, backed by the North Vietnamese government.

In 1964, the Gulf of Tonkin Resolution was passed by Congress at the urging of President Lyndon B. Johnson after U.S. destroyers in the Gulf of Tonkin allegedly were attacked by North Vietnamese torpedo boats. The resolution authorized the president to take action to defend U.S. forces and U.S. allies in South Vietnam. The U.S. air strikes against North Vietnam began in 1964 and U.S. troops eventually numbered about 550,000. The war was very unpopular among the U.S. citizens; strong domestic U.S. opposition to the war influenced the withdrawal of troops from the year of 1969, when peace talks began. With its own casualties mounting, the United States began transferring combat roles to the South Vietnamese troops in a process called Vietnamization. The Paris Peace Accords, a cease-fire agreement of January 27, 1973, formally recognized the sovereignty of both sides. Under the terms of the accords, all American combat soldiers were to withdraw by March 29, 1973.

Nevertheless, North Vietnamese military pressure against the South continued. In April 1975, the Saigon regime collapsed and the country fell to the Communists of the North. The Vietnamese Communists banned all other political parties, arrested public servants and military personnel of the Republic of Vietnam, and sent them to reeducation camps. The new government also embarked on a massive campaign to collective of farms and factories. Serious social, political, economic, and humanitarian setbacks created a huge refugee problem. The U.S. Congress promptly enacted special laws allowing Vietnamese political refugees to come to the United States. Between 1978 and 1979, tens of thousands of "boat people" from the South flooded the sea to flee from the Vietnamese Communists. At the height of these migrating waves, many "boat people" reached international waters where humanitarian ships from various countries would rescue and take them to refugee camps located in several Southeast Asian countries. Facing pressures from several international communities, the Communist government created guard posts along rivers and seashores to capture and incarcerate the so-called recreant citizens trying to escape.

Under the new Communist regime, life was hard, especially for those who were involved with the former South Vietnamese government. Ranked officers were sent to reeducation camps without knowing when they'd go home. As a former sergeant, our father was sent to a reeducation class, luckily just for a couple of months, to become a more productive citizen. He had to admit that he was not as productive as he would have liked to be, because he had to change from one job to another trying to support his family. Under the Communist rule, his children were not allowed to attend public university for higher education. In 1979, in a gutsy move, he sent one of my two older brothers onto one of the boats that carried people out to sea in search of a better life in another country. Unfortunately, river patrollers captured everybody on the boat and my brother was sent to jail for almost a year.

In 1980, with financial help from our grandparents, uncles, and aunts, our father bought a brand new fishing boat and out of nowhere became a fisherman. Our boat was not that big but she was the second biggest fishing boat in the village. We only went out to fish once every two or three weeks and our father did not seem to have a desire to make our boat lucrative. We consumed most of what we caught and gave away the rest to our neighbors. Our Catholic grandfather's baptized name was Peter, our father was a Peter and I was also a Peter, however, we were absolutely nowhere near being fishers like Peter of the Twelve Apostles. First, none of our relatives fished; therefore, we were not born as fishers. Traditionally, many jobs were to pass down from one generation to another in the same family. Secondly, we had no knowledge of fishing. Even though our father was always a tailor and all of us knew a little bit about threads and needles, shamefully we did not know how to make a fishnet or repair a torn one. Lucky for us, we did not rely for our living on fishing; otherwise, we would really have been in trouble. Lastly, our father probably had no desire to spend most of his life floating on the waters. Our father was not one for such a wandering life. To him, a boat was not a "home"; a house was a "home" where he could permanently live and raise his children.

Normal people just did not have the money to purchase a good-sized boat and let her sit at the port looking pretty. Local people knew that our father had something up his sleeve, because most fishing boats were smaller, usually about ten feet in length. However, nobody dared to gossip about it. Our father kept maintaining his position that he wanted to be a full-time fisherman someday. He did not divulge anything that could result in familial devastation. He acted the way that he was supposed to act, because with just one wrong move or word, he would put our whole family in jeopardy. Planning a covert escape was not even a machination. If caught doing so, everyone involved would be considered criminals and could be sent to jails and all their properties, including boats, houses, and lands, would be confiscated.

A year later, our boat became the biggest boat of the town by default. The family that owned the town's giant boat organized an escape and somehow word got out. In the middle of the night, the local authority came knocking on our front door. My family was scared, because we never had people banging on our front door after midnight. However, they only wanted to use our boat to go after the boat that was trying to flee the country. One of my brothers went to our boat with a whole bunch of these armed men and sent me — who'd been sleeping on the boat alone — home. They went and caught a whole bunch of those escapees, some of whom were the residents of our village. The officials then used some of the confiscated fuel to pay us for the boat rental. The next morning, our family — while doing our routines around town — was met with eyes that were filled with hatred. People thought that we had something to do with their loved ones' arrests, but our family did not even have a clue. We were just the innocent tools the officials used to perform their duty.

On November 29, 1983, my father, two brothers, and two sisters went to church at four o'clock in the morning. After the stroke of six, they arrived and met me at our boat to start the day just as if we normally went on a fishing trip. That fateful morning seemed a little colder than any other mornings. This day was one of those rare days that when I exhaled, my breath formed a visible column of fog, unusual and fascinating in the tropical region where the air temperature was fairly high year-round. The chilled air also explained why I did not hear any roosters crow. On any given day, roosters tended to have vocal contests to see which one would be having a date later. These roosters would go on and on; none seemed to give up, but today they were strangely quiet.

Many pedestrians walked with their arms folded in front of their chests, their shoulders raised high and their heads sunken. They walked quietly, straight ahead, and appeared wanting to get to their destination as quickly as they could. Many people, whose boats anchored close to ours had their stoves on. Each of the stoves had some kind of water kettles, for use in making coffee or tea. People gathered around fires to keep them warm, but all of them were very quiet, as if talking would cause them to lose all their bodily warmth. Things people normally did everyday today seemed so abnormal to me. Like a motion picture, everything seemed to be moving fast, but it was so vividly clear as if the film was in slow motion. My brain seemingly had been switched to a photographic mode that captured every single moment sound and movement. Now, all the usually irrelevant things of our daily lives suddenly became significant to me. I did not want to miss a thing, because deep down I knew I would not see them again.

I slept on our boat alone that night and waited for my family to arrive, then we all could abscond together. It never consciously occurred to me that once I left the village, I would not be returning. The feelings of leaving my loved ones behind, leaving the lands I grew up on and not knowing what would happen to me did not agonize me so much as having to leave the village in secrecy. Outside our family, nobody knew our plan to flee the country. It had to be a secret; otherwise, we would be arrested immediately for plotting to escape.

I did not even have a chance to say goodbye to my mother that morning. On the previous night, I did see one of my classmates and handed him an excused note written by my father asking the teachers to let me go on a family fishing trip for three days. If something held up our escape, I would be returning home in three days to resume my schooling. My father always had contingent plans. In addition to that, he always had some kind of notes written to my teachers whenever I needed to be absent from school, either because of sickness or other personal reasons. He had a great deal of respect for all of my teachers. Likewise, I had to respect all my teachers the same way I respected my parents, because they were second to my parents in serving as role models. Staying at home by herself, our mother was doing her normal work. That was to get up at three o'clock in the morning to make tofu. By the time all of us were on the boat; our mother was already at the market selling our fresh-made product. From the outside looking in at our family, everything seemed to be normal on this particular day.

The six of us had grim faces and seemed to have many things on our minds and we set sail without saying a word to each other. All of us knew that we had an important mission to accomplish. The small river was replete with boats carrying produce, livestock, and fish that were being taken to the marketplace. People seemed to be trying to beat the rush to get to the market before everyone else. Hustling voices from the vendors and yelping noises from live chickens and ducks signified yet another busy day, except for our family who motored slowly down the river without any hint of what we were about to endure.

Our father, along with my older brothers Tuan and Tu, my older sister Ly, my little sister Hue and I, navigated through the maze of rivers to get to the open sea — the South China Sea. There was no river map; therefore, we had to travel through endless rivers from memorization. The three or four times my father had taken our boat to the sea, he had hired a guide, a local experienced fisherman, who showed us what location to fish, from where we lived to the open sea. Learning to fish was not, however, the purpose of the hiring; looking for the shortest route to the sea without being searched by the authorities was the main intention. River patrollers stopped us once before we got to the saltwater. At that time, our father showed them all necessary travel passes and required permits. He had registered our boat to fish in the open sea and four crew members were legally allowed on the boat. We had two extra people, but from the outside looking in, we still looked like a normal family that was going on a fishing trip. Boats that sailed

The identification card of the author's father. At the top of the card it reads "Socialist Republic of Vietnam, Independence–Freedom–Happiness."

for the borders normally had more than six people onboard. This disguise surely allowed us to get through the inspection easily. In addition to that, at the checkpoint our father handed the venal officers some cash, "coffee and cigarette money" as we called it to discourage searching of our boat. Any thorough inspection could put us in a complicated situation if inspectors saw unreasonably large amount of supplies that could be used to escape from the country. Large amounts of fuel, water, and food would make us look so suspicious that we could be detained for questioning which could lead to imprisonment if we were found guilty of trying to escape.

When I was not able to see my own shadow as I stood upright, we had finally got through all of the branches of sinuous rivers and arrived at open water. We felt it right away as the water became a lot more turbulent. The wind sprang up a few notches; waves got bigger

Traveling permit issued by the Vietnamese Communist government allowing the author's father to operate his boat from his hometown to the open sea. The permit shows the boat being 8.6 meters long and 2 meters wide. The engine has ten horsepower. Capacity was four tons. Four crewmembers were allowed onboard.

and bigger; our boat rolled and pitched increasingly as we sailed away from smaller, calm rivers and through he estuary. As we distanced ourselves from the coastal lands, we felt our first shock of the sea.

Tu was strategizing about the course with Tuan who had one hand on the tiller. While sitting behind my standing brothers close to the stern where the tiller came up from the deck, I was nosily listening to their conversation. The wind was blowing strong as my two hands held firmly onto my seat so I would not be tossed into the water by the roller-coaster movement of the boat. Once in a while, water crashing against our vessel, along with a strong wind, created millions of fine water droplets that allowed me to taste and smell the sea in midair. While sitting there, I was completely captivated by the wind brushing my face and by the crashing waves against our boat out in the vast open space. I had never experienced anything like this before in my life. I felt like chains and cuffs that had held me down for so many years had finally come off to give me some sense of freedom. Moreover, this kind of freedom was within reach.

Our father was standing near the bow with one hand on the boat's tall, single mast, looking on. He turned his head and tossed his impeccable smile at us intermittently. His content smile was indicative of a roseate future, as if saying, "Sons, we are going to have good days ahead." His smile, with a flawlessly aligned set of white teeth against a dark- complexion weathered skin, always gave people a sense of peacefulness and truthfulness from an honest, hard-working family man. He had short black hair that never needed a comb but required a barber's maintenance once every two weeks. Barbershops were the places where married men hung out, played a game of Chinese chess, and talked about anything that was currently going on with their kids, their kids' schools, their jobs, their family businesses, their neighbors, and their society. The one thing they purposely did not discuss, even though tempting sometimes, was politics. This would have meant expressing various types of displeasure, but, lacking the freedom of speech, no citizens had the guts to criticize the government. People who lived in a Communist society normally lived within their own means. If they did not say or do anything "stupid"—outside government-proscribed norms—they would be fine. The norms meant that they did not have much, if any, freedom or human rights. People lived strictly by the codes that were set by the government and many times by laws loosely interpreted by local authorities. These authorities directed citizens what to do, and "good" citizens, such as our father, complied without hesitation or offering personal opinions. In a sense, citizens of a Communist country needed to behave like robots that were programmed by the government to perform tasks obediently that normal people would not do on their own. Our *free* citizens had as many human rights as prisoners do in the United States. The differences were that those U.S. inmates could still say whatever they wanted, and received free medical care and three meals a day; meanwhile, we could not say anything freely or get anything for free.

The hollow cheeks and bony face of our father did not represent the majority of the Vietnamese population, because most of the people normally had chubby cheeks and round faces. However, I believe our father would have had chubby cheeks if he had been fed a little better. He worked 365 days out of the year. Once every few years he also worked an extra day. On certain days, if he were lucky enough, he would get five hours of sleep. His typical twice-a-day meal mainly consisted of two small bowls of steamed rice, a couple pieces of salty dried fish, and some type of homegrown vegetables.

At mealtime, our whole family normally sat around the table and quietly ate at the same time. We did not talk much when eating. In fact, I would be reprimanded for eating and talking at the same time, because, as a kid, I tended to have food fly out of my mouth when I tried to chew and talk at the same time. That would be considered very inappropriate. But I wasn't the only one with this problem. Gathering for meals provided us with quality family time and an opportunity for everyone to consume some kind of warm food. Leftovers normally would be served cold, but we rarely had them, because without refrigeration they would be spoiled before the next meal. If anyone was not present at mealtime, he or she likely would go hungry until our next family meal; and that would be a long time, since we ate only two meals a day. As children at the table, we were not supposed to pick up our utensils and began to eat before our parents or any adults; this was to show respect to the elders. We always started to eat at the same time, but our father was normally the last one to finish. Not that he ate more than anyone else did, he just chewed his food slower than everybody else and claimed that his slow and thorough chewing would be good for his stomach and he would stay full longer. Once in a great while, our family could afford some poultry or meat, but he continued eating his vegetables and left the meat for us to eat, saying that vegetables were easier to digest. This was exactly what Ho Chi Minh had said to his people and his troops during the Vietnam War. Nevertheless, during hard times, eating foods at the bottom of the food chains seemed to be a wise choice. Truly, sometimes it was the only choice for us. Normally, our father would let us eat all the solid foodstuffs in a soup — the meat, chicken or shrimp, which we children *loved* to eat; he only consumed the broth, and said that the liquid had all the nutrients in it. We actually believed him, kept on eating what we liked to eat, and left him the liquids. But his abstemious habits did not fool anyone in the family. He was actually a gourmet whose eyes would light up when fine food was served. And, he was an interesting raconteur, with a defending story for almost everything. He always came up with a reason for his choice of action or behavior.

Dark gnarled skin, our father had such square shoulders that if he held a box up to them, his body would line up perfectly against the outline of the box. Some superstitious Vietnamese people believed that those square shoulders would denote his hard life. Culturally, Vietnamese people, mostly women, transported things around using two baskets, one tied to each end of a long bamboo stick. These pedestrians balanced the baskets by adjusting the bamboo stick on their shoulders and they could walk with one basket in the front and one in the back at a very good pace with a hefty load. This method of transportation stayed very close to the working-class people; and people with square shoulders would logically find this chore a lot easier, because the bamboo stick would be less likely to slip. Hence, whoever was born with square shoulders would be classified as a worker, expected to have a hard life. Our father fell into this category of hard-working people. He always tried to excel in all phases of his life to improve his own life and the lives of his children.

Slow water leaks in a wooden boat were normal but the amount of water leaking this time was an exigency; the inflow of saltwater filled our boat a lot faster than the times when we were on rivers. With concern, our father sent Tu down to inspect the boat for leaks. Tu found small round holes all over the bottom of the boat that had seawater squirting into the bilge just like water coming out from a whole bunch of drinking fountains. Parasitic worms, living in the river mud, which burrowed made their homes in the wood that happened to be our boat's structure, likely created these holes. The longer the boat sat in the mud, the more damage these critters would do. Those holes had still been sealed when we were at home; now the boat was under a lot more stress from the force of the crashing waves, and those holes opened, leaking water. With all these leaking holes, the correct way to repair them would be to bring the boat to dry land and then cork and patch them with tree sap. We did not have such a luxury at the time, but with urgency Tu was ingenious enough to cut some available bamboo chopsticks into short pieces and started to plug those holes. This was not part of our thoughtful plan, but the improvised chopstick plugs seemed to work very well under this circumstance. They perfectly fit into the holes and the dangerous water leak was minimized. While at the helm, Tuan pulled the little rope to activate the bilge water pump to get rid of the excess water weight.

Our boat, a small fishing vessel, had a bow, storage area with a sleeping space, engine compartment, steering area, and stern, all condensed approximately into a space of twenty-six feet long and seven feet wide at the belly. She was about six feet above the waterline at the bow. I could sit at the stern, which had the lowest deck, and touch the water without any difficulty. Our father added wooden boards to each of the two sides of the decks doubling the height to about three feet above the waterline. Even though she was small compared to many other boats, she was built to travel at sea. The bow was higher and narrower, used for breaking the ocean waves, than other normal river boats with bows lower and broader, yielding a flatter bottom which allowed them to transport more freight on rivers.

Our boat was totally made from wood, with interstices between wooden planks caulked with tree sap and secured with iron nails. Her shape was formed and held together by a set of pre-formed, curved wooden studs lining up systemically with spaces between them, making them look like a rib cage of a giant dinosaur. Originally, she was built as an open fishing boat with a small, covered cabin that housed the engine, the transmission, and the propeller shaft that ran through the bulkhead. Inside the cabin, an area seven feet wide by six feet long, removable floorboards almost completely covered all the mechanical components except for the transmission shifting stick and part of the high-rise exhaust pipe.

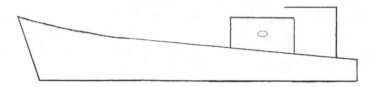

ORIGINAL OPEN FISHING BOAT WITHOUT MODIFICATIONS
(8 METERS LONG & 2 1/2 METERS WIDE)

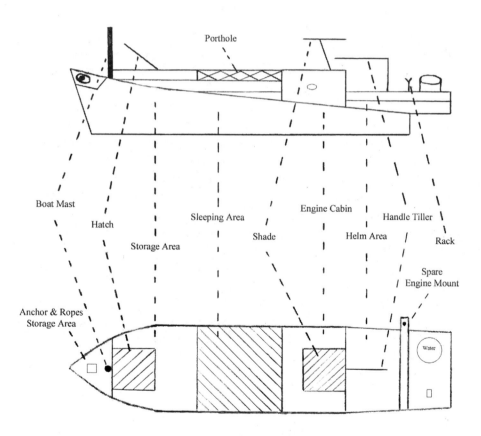

SIDEVIEW AND TOPVIEW OF THE BOAT WITH 1-METER EXTENSION

Plans of the boat, drawn by the author.

Our father had installed some corrugated sheet metals from some old sheds on top of the twelve-foot-long section in front of the engine cabin to keep the elements out of the hull. The sheet-metal roof next to the bow section of the boat contained a large hatch that could open to look like the hood of a car. This covered section was used to store supplies and to provide a resting place that was lined with wooden floorboards. Underneath the sleeping section — the belly, possibly the lowest part of the entire boat — our father had hidden a metal drum full of diesel fuel for this escape. This sleeping area had long, narrow portholes on both sides. I call these openings "portholes" but they were actually open windows that did not have any glass. These apertures were big enough for us to stick our hands through but not our heads. They were there for ventilation and they served as peepholes, allowing those inside to see outside.

Our boat was motored by a ten horse power, one-cylinder Yamaha diesel engine directly connecting to a modified transmission originally coming from an archaic Jeep or GMC front-end winch that had one backward gear, one neutral, and one forward. There was no clutch. To change gear, we had to lower the engine speed to almost dying. When the engine's was too fast, we could not change gears, and the grinding sound of the gears was not too pleasant to the ears. When the engine's speed was too low, the engine would die when the new gear was engaged. So, this gear-changing became almost a science to us, especially when we tried to dock our boat. We had to put the gear in neutral when we were approaching the dock. The forward momentum would take the boat to the dock and then at a precise moment, we would put the gear in reverse to stop the forward plowing of the boat. There were a few times that the engine died on reverse, causing our boat to slam into a riverbank or neighboring boats, creating havoc among those boats' occupants. The speed was low but the weight of the wooden boat gave her a lot of momentum at the point of collision. Sometimes bigger boats strike and capsize smaller ones, causing loss of lives and property. Fortunately, incidents like that never happened to us. Still, we hung some old car tires in the front and around our boat to give her some cushion in the event of crashing into somebody else's boat.

Some good-sized boats I knew of had steering wheels that came from a car or truck. Our boat did not have that luxury. Instead, we had a long wooden stick as our tiller handle that attached to the metal rod, sticking through the stern of the boat, which directly welded onto a metal rudder. Standing at the helm, the operator could use one of his legs to change gear, with one hand on the throttle control and the other one on the tiller handle. Cruising on the rivers, we just sat on top of the engine cabin to navigate. Large rivers afforded plenty of room to make mistakes without causing serious problems. To give the helm operator some protection from the rain and the greater light, there was a small rectangular sheet-metal shade bordered by wooden studs and held up by two wooden posts that were bracketed onto the roof of the engine cabin.

A second engine was mounted outside, on the starboard side, by the stern of the boat. This motor could be used as a spare in case the main engine broke down. This was a small two-stroke gasoline engine, similar to a push-lawn-mower engine, a couple of horsepower strong, which had a direct propeller shaft. Pulling on the rope would start the engine. Once the engine had started, simply submerging the propeller into the water would thrust the boat forward. When not in use this engine could be spun 180 degrees so that the propeller pointed straight forward and the propeller shaft rested on a metal hook on the side of the boat. We normally kept this engine inside the hull and took it out to test run periodically to ensure its service when needed. There was no doubt that this escape would need this kind of assurance. There were many known instances where overcrowded boats' engines broke down or the engines ran out of fuel, and "boat people" had floated on the sea for months. If lucky, some international ships would rescue these asylum seekers. Otherwise, they would certainly die from starvation and thirst after so many days without food and water.

Right at the stern of the boat there were two metal racks: one on each side. These racks were used to hold our fishnet with a dimension of fifteen feet in width, two feet in height, and twenty feet in length. The net had two metal plates — similar to a pair of skis — attached to the ends of a fifteen-foot-long piece of metal tubing. It was like a super stretched-out snowmobile that had nylon netting as its body and tail. The net was attached to a rope, which was tied to the mast of our boat. When in use, the net could be lowered to the bottom of a river. The boat could drag the fishnet on the riverbed. Fish then could be trapped at the tail end of the net. When the net got a little heavy, we could pull it up and empty the trapped contents onto the deck. These contents would contain all kinds of junk and among those useless articles, we hoped that we would find some fish and shrimp.

When we boated on rivers without choppy water, I normally did not get motion sickness. However, once we were sailing away from the estuary, I began to feel the soporific effect of the larger waves. This was probably the third time in my life on our boat near the rugged, open sea. I started getting nausea as if I was a man who had spent too many hours drinking at a bar. Seasick pills were not available so I decided to go inside where my two sisters were resting. When I saw them their faces were bloodlessly pale for they had been vomiting for quite sometime. They each had a bag in their hands and put their faces into these once every few minutes or so. What they threw up must have been the food we had eaten the night before, because none of us had eaten anything since we left home. From the unpleasant smell of their vomit the look on their faces, the engine-oil stuffiness of the air, and the unpredictable rolling motion of the boat, I felt worse instantly and started to vomit myself. I closed my mouth and looked around for a bag or a container of some sort to use. My eyes swiftly swept the area while my mouth was being pressurized. My bulging cheeks must have looked as if they were concealing two golf balls inside. The pressure built up intensely inside my mouth quickly to a point where my lips were not able to seal the contents any more then my mouth exploded like a water balloon that had stretched to its limit and popped. And I had thought that the vomits from my two sisters were gross. Mine landed on our sleeping area. Some got onto my sisters who normally would rebuke me for all I was worth. Some even landed on the ceiling, the sheet metal, and now dripped down like icicles that were melting away in a mountain cave during the summer. Nobody seemed to care at this point — as far as I could tell. I became exhausted, so I lay down on the wooden floorboard, face down, gagging and vomiting directly into the bilge water of the storage area.

While I lay down asleep, the unthinkable accident happened to our father who had gone down into the engine cabin to check on the bilge pump that had quit working. The flywheel of the diesel engine could directly drive the water pump — a small plastic type that looked similar to a regular swamp-cooler pump. When the flywheel spun, the engaging pump would empty the bilge water to the outside. Since we were at sea, our wooden boat had more water leaks than normal; the pump was running constantly to rid the unwanted weight back into the sea. If the pump went bad, we would have to dispose of all the bilge water by hand — not by hand pumps but with buckets. Usually when something failed to work, Tu—as the family mechanic — was the one who would go and check it out. However, this time, when the pump stopped working, instead of sending Tu or Tuan, our father decided to go down to the engine cabin himself while he was fighting a cold and wearing a jacket. There should be an answer out there to why our father went out of the ordinary to do what he did. Things always happened for a reason. First, there is a cause and then an effect follows. His decision to go down to check the water pump certainly had its own reason.

Our father was a very careful man who always preached and carried out safe practices throughout his entire life. At home, we had a diesel engine that powered a mill to extract juice from soybeans to make tofu; our father had shielded all the moving parts that posed potentially serious dangers. Somehow, Tu, one time, was caught by its drive shaft that plucked a big chunk of his long hair, along with a large patch of his scalp that resulted in a large scar producing a hairless spot. Since the accident, Tu usually wore a cap and tight clothing around machinery.

Not only could our father see potential dangers, he was always prepared for any accident. He always had his first aid kits available whenever we got hurt or our neighbors' kids got hurt. He never allowed us to ride a bike without a chain guard. If our bicycle did not have one, he would make one and install it himself. Many people walked around barefoot, but our father always demanded that we wear sandals or slippers and stay away from hazardous areas such as dumping grounds where broken glass and rusted sharp metal was common. One time, I stepped on a large piece of broken glass that went through my slippers and punctured deep into the bottom of my foot. I was bleeding ferociously while hobbling home on one leg. I left a trail of blood from the place of the accident all the way to our house. Our father immediately took me to the Catholic nuns, who worked as nurses and operated the only health-care center in the village, to give me a tetanus shot — a medical treatment that a normal villager generally would not get or could not afford. He did not care how much the shot cost, he wanted me to have peace of mind. I was so afraid to get that shot, but it was imperative that I have it, so the nurse gave me a choice of getting it on my thigh, where I could watch what she was doing, or on my behind. After thinking it over for one second, as a nine-year-old boy, I agreed to get that one on the butt.

Our father would not let me swim in the local river unless I had some type of floating device on my body. I could swim very well, but he did not want me to take chances since many good swimmers drowned between December and January every year in that river. It was said that the spirit of whoever died in that river had to pull somebody else down within the next year, so he or she could freely move on to reincarnate. Having a Catholic faith, our father did not believe in those tales; he was just cautious at whatever he and his children were doing. Therefore, our father must have been very careful when he went down to work around the running engine. He positively knew what kind of a risk it was to work around machinery. Maybe he knew it was a very dangerous job for my two brothers, so he had decided to do it himself. We just did not know.

With the combination of the strong water current, the howling winds, and the opportunistic waves, our troubled boat moved when the random touch of force applied, as if she was an abandoned vessel. After quick glance at the coastal landmass, I could see that she was slowly rolling, spinning, and going in a circle. While my brothers were still trying to free our father from the propeller shaft, another boat was heading straight toward us at a very fast speed. At first I thought it was a coast guard boat. My initial reaction was that we could use their help. Again, we could run into big trouble if they found out that we were trying to escape the country. I wanted it to be a government boat so badly and yet at same time I did not want it to be one. My wondering, confused mind was so contradictory at this moment. As the speedy boat approached ours, it turned out to be a larger fishing boat with a few men dressed in civilian clothes. It began circling ours as if it was a ravenous vulture ready to feed on carrion. I jumped up and down and waved both of my arms to signify that we had an emergency that required their immediate assistance. I cried out loud for help, "*Ba toi bi tai nan! Xin den giup chung toi.*" ("My father has had an accident! Please, come help us.") I did not know what was on their minds, but for sure they were not interested in helping us because they kept going around us while scrutinizing our situation. Higher than our boat, they could observe clearly and must have had a good understanding of what was going inside our boat, I thought. They must have noticed my two brothers who were trying very hard to free our father. Regardless, probably out of desperation, I put my hands together to form a bullhorn and screamed very loud to them that our father had gotten hurt and that we needed their help. I was sure that they heard my pleading. For some reason, these men, even with their eyes glued on us, were not about to offer us any help, by the expression on their faces. They did not talk to each other. They just stared at us. It was so strange. I had no clue what was on their minds. After several minutes of circling our boat for whatever reasons, they finally vanished into the openness of the sea. Then we were left alone.

My brothers finally cut loose the nylon jacket to free our father from the propeller shaft and carried him to our sleeping area. I immediately crawled back inside, via the engine cabin, to the adjacent area to join my siblings. All five of us knelt around our father in that confined space — seven feet wide by six feet long — without saying a word to each other. At this moment, none of us was trying to resuscitate our father, because we knew exactly what had struck us and what we were facing; unless the Lord God blew the breath of life into our father's nostrils right away. We were stunned. We were clueless. Then, all at once, we wept, as our God had taken our father home with Him. It was so soon, so early, and so sudden. Our father had not accomplished what he wanted for his life and for his family. He still had a wife at home waiting for his good news, and young children who still needed his love, care, and guidance. He had not brought us completely out of Vietnam to find a free land for our better future as he envisioned.

Settling in Australia — his ideal land of overflowing milk and honey — was my father's ultimate dream. He yearned to be a farmer on a big ranch where modern machinery was the mode of cultivation, not the backbreaking labor that he had endured for so many years of his life. That was his wish, he told me a couple of months before this escape, during a bicycle trip to Ho Chi Minh City. I cannot remember what the purpose of the trip was for him, but I believe he went to purchase something for our boat. At the same time, he had purchased me some mathematics books at a huge mall called Cho Ben Thanh, and I had saved enough change to buy myself an air gun that pumped out plastic caps.

After we paid some people to guard our bicycles at a designated large street divider, while heading to the mall on foot, we were enticed by an iced tea vendor. He showed us these huge, plastic cups of iced tea stacked on top of the cart. He said each cup would cost three Vietnamese dongs. The weather was hot and the iced tea looked so good; my father paid the vendor six dongs for two cups. After tucking his

Vietnamese currency: five dong and ten dong. Both bills together were worth about one U.S. dollar in 1983. These two bills were all the author's father had in his pocket when he died.

money away securely, the vendor proceeded to fill the cups that had been stacked behind the other ones. These cups were no doubt less than half the size of the mega-sized cups we'd seen. Of course, my father questioned the seemingly reasonable man, and his plain response — without any compunction — was that those large cups would cost five dongs each. It seemed like we were slapped in the face; but instead of getting into an imbroglio with the tricky vendor, my father just smiled, finished his drink, handed the mendacious man his cup, and walked away without looking back. I did the same and followed his lead.

Before we headed home for the day, we went to a restaurant to eat some noodles. The place looked very good compared to other places I had seen back home. While I ordered a cold, sweet fruit drink, my father wanted a cold, long-necked, Bia 33. Ensconced on a padded chair, he really enjoyed his drink. This was the first and only time I had seen him drink some kind of fermented beverage. At this time, he mentioned his dream to me that he wanted to live in Australia and to try out every single one of their beers. He handed his Bia 33 over to give me a sip, but I shook my head.

To help us enjoy our meal in the excessive heat, the clever waiter offered us some iced cold cotton towels with an additional cost. Right in the middle of the scorching summer heat, there was nothing better than a cold glass of iced tea, a sweating bottle of an iced cold beer, or an iced cold cotton towel to chill our faces and hands. My father was willing to pay extra for me to have that heavenly experience. Unfortunately, while I was eating, a customer sitting at the next table grabbed my precious towel before I had a chance to finish using it. I immediately turned around, but it was too late; the inconsiderate man already had it on his face. I was furious and ready to yell out "Sir, we paid for that!" but my father shook his head and hushed me before I could deliver contumelies. Then, gladly, he gave up his own towel for me to use. We finished our meals and quietly left the restaurant without raising any commotion.

Besides a broken right arm and an abrasion near his right temple, our father did not have a single drop of blood on his body. He lay there with his eyes closed, looking so peaceful, as if he was taking a nap. My brothers believed, plausibly, that a rogue wave knocked our father off balance while he was trying to fix the water pump. As physically weak as he was while fighting a cold, he may have slipped; parts of his unzipped jacket were tangled onto a bolt of the U-joints of the propeller shaft. The revolving shaft wound up his jacket pulling him down, causing his right temple to strike hard against the transmission, knocking him unconscious, and breaking his right arm. The full-throttle engine was jammed and just stopped cold. The whole incident happened perhaps as fast as the shutter speed of a camera. It was like a well-thought plan that only God knew about. We as humans only played a very insignificant role in His mystical intention. To us, it was very vague; therefore we called this whole incident an "accident" because we had no control over its occurrence. Things happened for a reason and we simply did not know what reason that was.

The uncontrolled rolling and pitching of the boat, the whirling of the vessel, the sound of the splashing waves, and the hissing wind rushing through the portholes were so relevant, but they had been tuned out by all of us. The only sounds we heard at this point were our own intermittent sobbing and our own heartbeats and heavy breathing, now one less onboard than a few minutes ago. We were speechless. We felt completely bereft because we had just lost our love, our leader, our captain, our decision maker, and ultimately our giver of life. Nevertheless, the inevitable question arose in a hurry as to what we were going to do now that our plans had been seemingly thwarted by forces that were beyond us.

While there was still daylight and coastal land was still vaguely visible, our first option was to turn around and go back home to face unknown consequences. This option would likely allow us to get home by early next morning, to bury our beloved father and to grieve over him for a long time. This option would also mean killing our father's dream and hope of having us — his children — grow up in a free society, because we did not know if we would ever have another chance of setting sail again. This choice appeared to be the easiest and made the most common sense, since our father was no longer with us to lead the way. The second option was to execute our plan, to continue our escape without the benefit of our father's knowledge and experience. This choice appeared to be risky, since none of us had any precise idea of what we would be doing and facing. Our father did discuss the proposed journey with my two brothers briefly at home. However, what they had talked over was dos and don'ts based on information our father had gathered from people who had escaped successfully to freedom. It was without a doubt that we needed our father's presence in order for us to be successful.

What would my father have done if one of his children had died on this trip? I sincerely believed that out of the love for his child he would definitely return back home, bury his child, and grieve for a long time over his lost love regardless of what would happen to him. One time my father and I were on the same bicycle returning home from a long day of farming. I was sitting on the crossbar in front of him; the back seat had some produce on it. We were going downhill and suddenly we hit a deep pothole; these were present everywhere since the road was unpaved. My left foot swung and happened to stick between the bicycle's front fork and the front tire's spokes. The front wheel got jammed. The sudden stop of the front wheel flipped our bicycle into the air and we both went airborne too. My father landed and rolled ten or fifteen feet away from me. Then the bicycle came down and landed right on top of me. While lying on the ground and groaning in pain, with a blurry vision, I saw a thin figure that rose up quickly, rushed to my side, tossed the bicycle aside, picked me up, and carried me almost a mile to the Catholic nuns' medical facility as if in one breath. After all was said and done, I got a slight headache — possibly a concussion — and some abrasions on my elbows, knees, and feet. I was easily treated with a couple of bandages. In contrast, my father received more cloth wraps and bandages on his body and face than I could count. Still, I leaned on him while we were both limping home together. Before we made it home, he mentioned how he used his former parachuting experience to land safely, which explained why he was tossed and rolled a lot farther than I. In my heart, I knew that he did what he could so that he would not land on top of me. We both shared a good laugh as we arrived at our house where somebody had already placed our bicycle — which had the front wheel bent — at our front door.

"*Bay gio, minh tiep tuc di hay quay ve?*" ("do we continue, or go home?") asked Tuan, while we all still circled our father. I glanced through the portholes and saw the greater light starting to set. The waves moved our boat up and down rhythmically. Every time we were at the top of the waves, I vaguely saw a long stretch of land in the far distance. Nobody propounded any ideas. Everybody was quiet. It appeared that everybody was waiting for words from somebody else. We looked into one another's eyes to search for an answer. Who among the five would make this decision of life or death, of now or never? It was like we were playing a game called "Who has more patience?" and that whoever talked first would lose. Several minutes passed and they seemed like eternity. It was as if we were standing in the middle of a three-way intersection and we had to pick a correct road. One road would take us home to face the uncertainties; one would tragically lead us to death at sea; and the last one would lead us safely to freedom.

Suddenly, without any words, Tu got on his feet, cranked up the engine, slipped out of the engine compartment, grabbed the tiller handle, shifted the gear forward, and put the throttle on full. All inscrutable actions seemed to be in one deft move with a pure determination. The four of us just sat still, sobbed, and watched Tu do his mysterious things. Still shocked from what happened to all of us, I looked through the engine compartment toward the back of the boat and realized that we were sailing away from Ba Ria Mountain, the most prominent feature of Vung Tau Beach. Nobody said anything. Tu's momentous decision, for us to continue as planned, had granted him a new role — our father's role — as leader of the pack. Not that we all agreed with his adamant decision or thought that his choice was the correct one, but none of us was strong or wise enough to decide someone else's fate. Tuan was two years older than Tu, but he, with an attitude of insouciance, was a quiet, perfunctory passive type of person who always waited for someone else to make decisions for him and he would just sit there and collect his harvest afterward. If the decision had been left to my two sisters and I, we would have returned home, regardless of any difficulty we were going to face. Our beloved father meant a whole world to us; he was like a heart of a living thing, a king of a castle, a commander of an army, a locomotive of a train, and an integral chip of a computer; once he was gone, that was the end of it. All we really wanted to do was to take our beloved father home, bury him, and grieve over him for a long time. That was the easiest and quickest way out of this difficult situation. We certainly wanted to do what any other normal person would have done. Tu surely was a maverick; he had his own reason for us to continue. In addition, none of us showed any sign — physically or verbally — against his decision at this moment.

While Tu was at the helm, Tuan told us that we should say a rosary for our beloved father. We nodded. With our heads bowed and hands clasped, we started to pray. We looked up to the three wallet-sized pictures my father had taped underneath the rooftop right above our heads. These were pictures of our Lord Jesus Christ, our Lady of Perpetual Help, and Saint Peter of the Apostles. Our father placed those pictures there when we first got our boat. A local priest had blessed them all. I was always taught that Jesus was our Savior. He was the One who could move mountains, calm storms, cure the sick, and give life to the dead. Mother of God meanwhile would help the least fortunate and the outcast of human society. She would come to deliver hope and comfort to God's faithful ones who were in absolute despair and needed new direction in life. Saint Peter the fisherman, of course, was our patron saint. We prayed to God that with the little faith we had, He would allow us to walk on water as Saint Peter did once, according to Matthew. Everything was possible with God. While praying for the soul of Peter, we were asking the graceful God, along with His saints and angels, to watch upon us, His little children, and deliver us from the raging sea. Looking at those pictures gave us a lot of comfort and hope since the holy ones gazed down with love and concern.

Everyday, we absolutely had to do one thing as a family, according to our parents; that was to have our evening prayer together under a small altar with a flickering oil lamp. Praying together as a family not only brought us closer to God and reduced our temptation to do bad things, but it also allowed us to build a stronger bond among our family members. Family gatherings to have an evening prayer were not too hard, since we all went to bed early because there was not that much entertainment in the village when nighttime came. Our way of life was much like the Amish way of life. The only difference was that the Amish chose their lifestyle and we were forced to live such a way in a Communist society.

Without electricity, the streets and most houses were pitch-black after dusk. Before 1975, when our father still served in the military and our family lived in Saigon, this village, Phuoc Ly, thrived because of its proximity to a large military base, Thanh Ty Ha, and a special military canine training facility, Quan Khuyen. At the village's only river bridge, a huge electric generator supplied power for all residences of the town. After the war, some people came, disassembled the whole generator, and shipped it to the North, leaving our whole town in the dark. The remnants left behind were street power poles spaced at fifty yards or so, and there was one standing right in front of our house. Hung was my best friend. At six residences away from us, his house also had a pole in front. His front yard had a large tamarind fruit tree that over the years grew so much it shielded the whole power pole from being seen. Every year during the harvesting season, Hung and I, with a whole bunch of neighbor kids, would hang out on that tree trying to pick the juiciest and the biggest fruit so we could brag about it all day long. It happened on one day that I accidentally slipped from a small branch while trying to reach for my prized pick of the day. On the way down to my sure death upon impact with the ground, by the grace of God, I miraculously grabbed onto of one of the four copper electric wires between the two poles. For dear life, I hang on tightly to the wires and inched my way to safety. After the incident, I learned my lesson and completely stopped climbing on tall trees. This incident was almost deadly but I was fortunate, a few months after that, those copper wires were gone due to some thieves who liked to recycle the precious metal. Surely, I had been blessed.

Living in a small town, we had only a few coffee shops where young men and women could hang out in the evening. These customers probably didn't care how much light was in the shops. To them, the darker it got, the better it was, which I did not then know. Other places young people could go were billiard shops where pool tables were lighted by small, short fluorescent lamps powered by portable rechargeable batteries that could be taken to a recharging shop everyday for reenergizing. But our parents were very strict; they would not allow us to hang out late at night. Normally we could not afford to be in such places. In addition, most unwanted social issues could arise in those places, according to our parents. Our daily routine was very simple; a short time after supper, we would have our family evening prayer. If we had any homework from the school, we had to do it under the dim light of an oil lamp. I usually did mine right after school during daylight. There was no television, so we did not have to worry about watching it too much. Only a handful of affluent families in the village owned a television. Occasionally, I would stand outside their windows to have a glimpse of what was showing in black and white. That was as close as I could get to a television set. Then all lights were out by eight or nine o'clock every single night. That was our way of life.

Lately, our prayers had been seriously long because our father's father had passed away, three months before our escape, after a battle with chronic liver disease. Our extra prayers were offered to God for the soul of Peter. At this moment our thoughts and prayers for our father's soul, also a Peter, went smoothly, fluently, and loudly — they penetrated the eerie night and suppressed the ever-powerful quakes of the angry sea. I believed that our pleading voices had reached heaven that night, without a doubt. I was sure that our living God was listening to our every single word.

When gloaming arrived, while our prayers were still going on, Tuan lighted our wind-proof kerosene hurricane lantern and hung it on a half-embedded nail from the rooftop of the engine cabin. There was not much, but there was light. The yellow flickering flame from the lantern, partially tunneled through the small cabin door, cast a lifeless color on each one of our worried and exhausted faces. It cast our shadows on the walls of the boat. The shadows looked so strange as the lantern swung back and forth due to the roughness of the sea. These irregular shadows gave me a feeling of swimming alone in a lighted swimming pool in the middle of the night; and the constant shape changes of the shadows on the walls of the boat gave me a creepy feeling of being watched right in the middle of the sea. Who else was out there besides our father and the five of us?

We ended our prayers with a familiar, dear-to-the-heart "Ave Maria" hymn. Our upbeat singing speared through the darkness of the night. It was like a floating beacon that sent out a signal of our faithful hearts and souls. Our voices dissipated into a vast, dark, empty space but they were so warm and comforting within the confinement of our little boat. Tu, steering the boat outside, even sang along with us. All five hearts united as one. The winds, the waves, and the rocking of the boat occasionally muffled our individual voices, but when these interrupting forces passed, we found ourselves singing harmoniously as if nothing had disturbed our unity.

Tu's noticeable singing was a little bit unusual because during our evening prayers, he normally murmured to himself when all of us prayed aloud. Singing hymns, without a rehearsal or a written material, seemed to be so natural to us, since all of us except my little sister had joined our church chorus at one time or another. During my times serving as an altar boy, there were more than ten of us available — all boys — who could assist our priest during mass, which required only two per mass. After each Saturday afternoon mass, Di Ut, a nun, would appoint two of us to serve the following week starting on the next day. I loved being an altar boy when there was a wedding in the church. Most of the times, the altar boys would receive some monetary gift from the wedding couple's families and an invitation to their sumptuous feast. We little boys loved that.

During the weeks when we were not assisting the priest, we were asked to join the chorus, which normally consisted of older singles who now — during the difficult time — usually worked long hours for a living and could not come to the four o'clock weekday masses. Chorus leader Chi Le always had a difficult time teaching us young boys how to sing, because none of us was born with a naturally fine singing voice. By the grace of God, we tried. In addition to that, Chi Le had a God-given talent and energy for running the church chorus daily without any compensation. She played on an antique piano that had a mechanical pedal that required constant foot pumping actions in order for it to spit out any sound. I had heard that this piano had been in the church since the missionary French built it in the 1920s and we had not been able to keep up with modern technology.

Before each daily mass, this hilltop church's humongous bell tolled for a long time to notify churchgoers to gather. The bell's penetrating toll could be heard loud and clear throughout the town. Many families did not have sundials to tell time, they relied solely on the church's bell to time their daily routine. When someone within our church community died, family members would notify the priest and someone would immediately toll the bell seven times for a deceased male or nine for a female. Villagers then ran around the neighborhood to find out who had just passed away, so they could offer a prayer or pay the mourning family a visit. This huge bell was so heavy that only strong, heavy adults were physically able to pull and move the steel chain wrapped around a huge wheel along with the bell that attached to a horizontal bar. When the repeated pulling and releasing of the chain applied enough momentum, the bell would swing back and forth to a point where the inside hammer would strike it.

Along with some friends, I usually hung around the church area during hot summer days to keep cool. Actually this was the second favorite area; our first choice was swimming in the river. It was a good spot because it was situated high up and faced the vast open area of the rice fields of the east where seasonal winds came from. We loved lying on the concrete and red-brick floor underneath the tower, watching the bell and listening to the soothing sound produced from the breeze that entered through the decorated crevices of the tower. We talked, relaxed, and sometimes fell asleep for a while. As children, we acted puerile sometimes, three or four of us pulling the bell chain together to toll the bell. By hanging on to the chain, all of us could go airborne without any problems. When the hammer struck, all of us ran away confusingly in different directions before one of the two nuns could come out and identify us.

I believe we did this child's play, not disrespecting the nuns, but to return something to them. These two nuns were something. Di Ut was okay; she only smacked us once in while for talking in church. However, Di Tam, older, was the one we wanted to have fun with. I believed that Di Tam was at least one hundred twenty years old; she could very well have been the oldest nun alive. Her bloodshot eyes always looked so scary that none of us had the guts to look at her directly. She always had this inch-thick pair of eyeglasses on, but when she looked at us she never looked through her glasses. She bowed her head a little and looked at us over the top, outside edges of her glasses. If I had been brave enough to look her in the eye, I would have been able to see all the individual red veins that were grabbing her eyeballs. We went to her residence for catechism classes, but there was no classroom. We, the students, had to sit on the floor in a large, main hallway with our backs against the two bare concrete walls. Sometimes we were tired and needed to stretch our legs. If that happened, Di Tam was sure to walk by and get tripped up by one of those outstretched legs. I felt sorry for whoever's leg that was, because it had happened to me a couple of times. At the same time, I was glad one time that it was not me, because she showed no signs of decrepitude and did not even bother to castigate the boy; she simply raised her legs and repeatedly kicked that poor boy as if she was a World Wrestling Entertainment wrestler trashing her helpless opponent in a fetal position inside the ring. When that happened, the rest of us just covered our faces with books, pretending to be reading, because if she caught any of us staring at her while she was having such a good time, she would switch to a new opponent, and none of us wanted to be her next victim.

When we did not know our homework, the punishment was as harsh as that of a spy being interrogated by enemies. Oral exams were not merely difficult, but onerous to us, the young, refractory students, who loved to play and ignore homework. Occasionally, I did not study and memorize my assignment. I then decided to skip classes for that day, because I did not want flagellation on my open palm with a wooden ruler from the intransigent nuns. Having the ruler break while receiving our punishment was the worst thing that could ever happen to us. The teacher had to go find another ruler and in the process she would lose count of our punishment; always this meant restarting her count with her new weapon. This explains why we had to skip classes if we did not study. But the town was small and word got around. My father found out sometimes and spanked me hard at home for unexcused absences. I would never get a spanking for anything else. Mentally, it hurt more when my beloved father disciplined me. Either way, I would be punished physically, so I listened to my father, went to my classes, bit my lip, and learned to have the votaries discipline me instead.

These nuns were also known for something else. Most homes raised domestic animals that would consume the family's daily leftover food, so that the food would not become a waste. When these animals matured, they became either a family's next meals or extra income if they were sold to someone else. Our family always had a few poultries to slaughter during our Tet (New Year's) celebration. The nuns also owned a whole bunch of them, chickens and ducks, as well as pigs. We students became their caretakers, from preparing their foods to washing them and cleaning their scats. During our recess, we had to go out digging up earthworms to feed the nuns' chickens and ducks. These animals were not as gentle as the ones we had at home. They would chase and attack us for no apparent reason. Luckily for me, I did not have to tend these annoying pets too much, largely, I think, because of the nuns' opinions of my father. The most I had to do for these two nuns was to sweep the floors, dust the furniture, and polish brass candleholders and lamps for the church. Every Tet, and on many other holidays, due to my father's wishes, I always walked with him to pay these nuns a visit and offer them some traditional gifts. Not that my father could easily afford this thoughtful munificence, and other people did not, but my father had a great deal of respect for these nuns, and he liked to show his gratitude tangibly. My father had laid that foundation but these God-fearing teachers still treated me abnormally. However, in my mind, I was not being treated as badly as some other boys who probably got the worst from these nuns. I was just glad that I was not one of those boys. This sounds cruel and abusive, but culturally it was very normal and acceptable at the time, when these nuns earned respect from our parents and we children had to learn to be submissive and to do whatever we were told.

Tet was definitely the most celebrated time of the year. We lived day-to-day, but Tet was what we all looked forward to every single year. During December of the lunar calendar, people fixed up their houses with new paint and new furniture. They dressed up their homes with beautiful flowers and colorful decorations. Everybody seemed to save money throughout the whole year just to spend for the first few days of the new year. Most people would celebrate three or four days. However, wealthy people would extend their celebration ten days and beyond. During those days, people stopped working and schooling, which allowed them to pay visits — in town or out of town — to relatives and friends. As kids, we had a chance to wear a new set of clothes and had our photos taken. Most of us did not celebrate our actual birthdays so Tet turned us a year older. We went and wished elders a happy new year. By sending out those wishes, we were awarded with money that was kept in a red paper envelope. The more we children did it, the merrier we were. We then used the money to gamble — always on the streets — for three straight days.

The water was relatively calm based on where we were on the open sea. Our boat pitched and rolled as if we were sitting on a kiddie roller coaster ride taking us through a series small hills and valleys. She was commandingly on full throttle, straight ahead, according to our strategic plan which was researched, studied, and written down by our father. Since he was no longer with us, we had to execute his plan without the benefit of his wisdom when we faced the unexpected. Without a doubt, my brothers were so physically and mentally strong that they were full of determination to take this little boat to the land of the free.

While my two brothers took turns keeping the boat on course, my two sisters and I fell asleep next to our beloved father. Throughout the night, our sleep was interrupted intermittently by the rolls of the boat and by the loud booms from our boat's collision with the water. My sisters and I kept rolling onto each other and waking each other up. Our father lay there unfazed — his body had turned cold and stiff. We were all tired from being seasick but none of us could fall into a deep sleep. In addition to the sickness, fears of awaiting dangers and anxieties from anticipation had mentally worn us out a lot more than had the absorption of the physical beating from the sea.

The boat my brothers were operating did not have any modern, state-of-the-art equipment. As a matter of fact, for sea travel, she had very limited equipment. Our critically important directional bearing was solely dependent on an old military compass owned by my father when he served in the military before 1975. Sea compasses were not available at the time, so we used what we had. We also had an out-dated Southeast Asian regional map that had been folded so many times that when unfolded an odor of old paper was given off. The folded edges had worn to the point where we had to open the map with a lot of care, otherwise the map ripped apart into smaller rectangular pieces. I believe it was a color map when new but by now all colors had faded light and dark were the only distinguishing characteristics. We had a four-D-cell, battery-operated metal flashlight — a piece of equipment that was considered luxurious by most where we lived, but which to us was a necessity during this escape. Batteries were expensive and most people could not afford this luxury when placing food on the table was the main purpose of every day's drudgery. Another source of light we had was an overused kerosene hurricane lantern, which we'd had on the boat for a long time. Over the years, it had collected all kinds of grime and engine oil that now seemed responsible for holding the lantern together. The glass globe contained a thick layer of black soot that was so concentrated near the chimney that no light was allowed to be emitted there. The lantern was only half as bright as it would have been if cleaned. But every time we disassembled the lantern to clean the globe, it broke. The globe was made of super thin glass which over time was subjected to hot flames that perhaps it so fragile. We just stopped taking it apart to clean after a while, which made it look like an antique.

We had a first-aid kit that contained a bottle of hydrogen perox-ide for cleaning open wounds, some clean cloths, a few bandages, a tube of antibiotic cream, a pair of scissors, a bottle of liquid iodine, a bottle of analgesic balm, and a bottle of aspirin. I grew up knowing only aspirin that everybody took when they had a fever, cold, headache, stomachache, muscle pain, or anything in between. Aspirin was the panacea that every family had, so it was not surprising that we had a bottle in our first-aid kit. The sad thing about aspirin was that people taking a lot of this medicine started having stomach problems later in their lives. By the time the side effects showed up, irreversible damages had already been done. Unfortunately, everybody knew of the side effects but just did not have other alternatives to choose. Analgesic balm was another universal medicine that was used extensively in conjunction with the aspirins to cure different illnesses. People would rub this menthol oil on different parts of their bodies and then use a tool — preferably an old coin — to strike back and forth against the skin until red bruises showed up. This traditional remedy was supposed to relieve any pain or ache the patient was experiencing. Some people still use this technique in America. As a result, their bruises have been mistaken for injuries suffered at the hands of another person.

We had a metal toolbox that contained some of the most common tools. A hammer, a few screwdrivers, a couple of pairs of pliers, an adjustable wrench, and a set of metric wrenches seemed to be the main tools inside that small, rusted container.

Underneath the floorboard where we slept, our father had hid a full fifty-five-gallon metal drum of diesel fuel. This much fuel was considered excessive, hence illegal. Under the government's regulation, only a small amount of fuel, enough for a fishing trip, was allowed onboard. Any excessive fuel indicated, according to the law enforcement, that the boat could be heading for the border, trying to transfer the questionable fuel to another boat that was trying to escape the country, or selling the fuel in another location for profit, something that was regarded as "illegal smuggling."

An oil-burning stove was another piece of luxurious and convenient equipment that we had for this escape. Most people used the more economical wood-burning stoves at homes and on boats. Oil usage could be very expensive to the common people, since oil was an import commodity. Woods were an easier-to-acquire alternative. People simply went to the jungles and chopped down some trees. At first, logs were huge, so people needed to split them several times before they would be able to be used in their stoves. After a while, those fire logs got smaller and smaller, and then finally they all looked like branches that did not require splitting anymore. At home, we mostly used rubber trees' hard nut shells and cellulose rice hulls as cooking fuel. We collected those rubber nutshells from a rubber plantation, purchased rice hulls from rice mills, and used a special stove to burn them. The hurricane lantern and the stove would be useless without a fire starter, therefore we had one Bic butane lighter and three boxes of matches. We kept these separately in different plastic bags to ensure their functionality when needed. We also had some pots, pans, bowls, and utensils onboard for cooking and eating.

Drinking water was the most important supply besides the fuel. On a normal fishing trip, we had five five-gallon plastic jugs of drinking water that would last us for more than a week, but we had never gone for more than three or four days. This difficult escape was surely replete with uncertainties; our father had added a small drinking-water barrel, which was securely strapped down onto the rear extension section of the stern. If used correctly, this fresh water, tripling the total amount we had onboard, would last us for months at sea.

Rice was our main choice of food. We had a large plastic container full of rice sitting in the supply area in front of where we slept. This was the first time I saw this much rice in our family, either at home or on the boat. At home, we normally bought a few liters of rice at a time, which would last us a few days. Normal households purchased their food daily; a lot of people worked, made money, and used that money to buy their daily bread. The next day, the arduous cycle repeated itself. These less fortunate people lived day to day; to them there was no tomorrow. Of course, there were people who were better off financially, but still had to buy food daily because there was a lack of refrigeration.

Besides the rice, we also had some fresh vegetables, dried fish, fish sauce, soy sauce, salt, sugar, and cooking oil that would enhance the taste of plain steamed rice. In case we needed some extra food, we could use our fishing poles to catch fish by using a jarful of earthworms our father had asked me the night before to dig up from the dirt around our papaya trees. According to our father, keeping our fishnet onboard would be advantageous, but the great depth of seawater could pose a problem. Still, it was there to serve as a security blanket. Our father had proclaimed that he would make sure we would not run out of the three most important things: fuel, water, and food. Besides these three vital things, everything else was just icing on the cake as far as he was concerned.

When reaching new lands, a new obstacle we would be facing was communication with the local people. Speaking or understanding their languages would be ideal. To us, a Vietnamese-English dictionary was all we needed for the escape — with the assumption that most learned individuals of the free world would be able to communicate in English. If we also knew one or two Chinese dialects, we would be okay for traveling throughout the Southeast Asian region where people of Chinese descent were well represented. I admired these Chinese people. Wherever they were, they grouped together, they helped each other out, they did businesses together, they maintained their culture and loyalty for each other, and ultimately they all succeeded together. I had a few Chinese classmates at home whose families were very wealthy from doing businesses. They kept to themselves, stayed within their own community, and spoke their own language with each other. But back at home, there was no need for me to learn their language, because these Chinese spoke mine.

We did not bring any extra blankets for the trip. We only had an army blanket that we rarely used due to the normally hot temperature in Vietnam. The only time we might need a blanket was likely right before sunrise when temperatures supposedly dipped to the lowest of the day. I always slept on top of the blanket — maybe I liked the little cushioning it offered on the hard wooden bed, and when the temperature was a little cold I slept in a fetal position, hugging my huge pillow, with the blanket still underneath. Tuan always said that I was dumb for doing that; maybe I was, but that was how I always slept. Other than that, a wooden bed, without a mattress, would have only pillows and a mosquito net to prevent malaria.

Plasmodium, parasitic protozoa — transmitted by the bite of female anopheles mosquitoes — cause malaria. Once in human red blood cells, these parasites divide up to twenty-four daughter cells. After destroying these red blood cells, parasitic cells enter the plasma and infect other blood cells. Infection causes fever, chills, sweating, and other severe complications that can lead to death. In Vietnam, mosquitoes were like bloodhounds; even sleeping under a net, I always would be able find a few of them, fully fed, inside the net in the morning. People used all kinds of means, such as eliminating standing water and using toxic DDT's (banned in most countries), to minimize their propagation. Still, the dangerous mosquitoes thrived, threatening the life of every single human being in warm-weather regions. I had my share of acquaintances contracting this highly publicized pestilence, as often as the change of the week. Infected people were sent to out-of-town hospitals with shivering colds and sometimes returned home dead — the same day. It was scary, an unpleasant fact, that everyone had to live with.

Our father told us to pack a few items of old clothes and to leave all good ones at home. At the time, I did not know why he gave us this directive, but later our generous mother gave our clothes to less fortunate neighbors. I personally did not own many clothes; a few pairs of shorts and pants and some short-sleeve shirts were all I had. I always took a bath in the evening, hand-washed my dirty clothes at the same time, and hung the fabrics out to dry, to wear the next day. In school, I had to wear a uniform: a white shirt and a blue pair of pants. Along with these, I had to wear a red neckerchief, a requirement for all students to be allowed into the schoolyard. This red neckwear was promoted the youth movement of the Communist Party.

Besides regular clothes, there was one set — a white, long-sleeve shirt and a pair of black pants — that I wore solely for church. We were not wealthy but when we were going to church we looked as good as anybody else. My father always reminded me that going to church was just like going to see my grandparents; both required appropriate dress. As a boy in the hot humid conditions, I normally wore a pair of shorts and remained shirtless at home. Nevertheless, before all our evening prayers no matter how hot it was, shirts were put on. Often while we were praying our sweat was dripping down as if we had just got out of the shower. My father would not let us use hand fans too much to keep cool because he said the commotion was just too distracting while praying. After the praying session, I literally had to peel my thighs off the aluminum chair, like a bandage coming off skin, to go outside for a cool-off before going to bed. Those hot days tended to put me to sleep while praying. I loved to sit toward the back of the room and learned to move my lips while napping. Somehow, I always woke up on time for the final hymn that required standing. My father later found out about my misbehavior and made me sit right in front of him during our evening prayers. I got quite a few smacks on the head every time I started nodding.

Beside all the supplies specifically for the escape, there were plenty of other household items, on our boat which would allow us to survive for months at sea if necessary, according to our father. Even though our boat was small to travel at sea, it had ample room for all of us and she stayed afloat fairly well. There were boats the same size or smaller that had carried up to a hundred "boat people" across the sea. We had heard horrible stories about unfortunate people who spent weeks and sometimes months at sea without food and water. Unexpected things — like too many people onboard, not enough supplies to start out with, and mechanical failures — were the main troubles these people had faced. Many died as the result of thirst or starvation. We had the whole boat to ourselves, so our basic needs of fuel, food, and water were the last things we had to be worried about. As long as she stayed afloat, we were going to be okay for months.

In front of where we stood to navigate our boat, the compass was held down by two big rubber bands, coming from the crosscut of a motorcycle tire inner tube and looking like calamari rings, stretched out by two rusted nails embedded directly into the wooden roof of the engine cabin. The pragmatic plan to reach our destination was very plain and simple. As soon as we met the sea, we were going to sail straight out away from the land until no land was within sight. We would keep the same direction for half a day to make sure we were clear of Vietnam's coastal lands and islands completely before we would turn 120 degrees southeast for three days and three nights. We then would turn sixty degrees northeast until we reached land. According to these coordinates, we would go around Con Dao Island, pass Mui Ca Mau, the south tip of Vietnam, avoid the Gulf of Thailand, and likely reach one of two free countries Malaysia or Indonesia — in five or six days. We had learned that there were several refugee camps located in those two countries and run by the United Nations High Commission for Refugees — and that they would open welcoming arms to temporarily accept Vietnamese refugees who would then apply to be resettled in other free countries, such as Australia, Canada, the United States, and some European nations.

Our first targeted destination was the Southeast Asian country of Malaysia. The first Vietnamese "boat people" arrived on the east coast of Malaysia in May 1975, right after the Communists of the North began taking over the South. They were the first of a large wave of people who fled to neighboring countries in the successive Communist victories in Vietnam, Cambodia, and Laos. Over 250,000 boat people were given temporary asylum in several camps in Malaysia, where they were under the care of the UN High Commission for Refugees, the Malaysian government, and the Malaysian Red Crescent Society. Almost all of them were resettled in western countries but about 9,000 had to return safely back to Vietnam by 2005 due to the closure of all refugee camps in Malaysia. These 9,000 people were not given the status of political refugees; all countries had denied their asylum-seeking wishes.

With the same planned course, we would reach some islands of Indonesia — our second choice of destination — depending on factors such as overall wind directions, water currents, drift factor, and the speed of our boat. The island of Galang in Indonesia had a refugee camp that accommodated 147,000 Indochinese refugees from 1979 to 1996. Galang Refugee Camp had a camp administration office, a Red Cross hospital, and the UN High Commission for Refugees offices. Many nongovernmental organizations like Save the Children also opened and taught grade schools to children in the camp. The main activity for all refugees was the study of foreign languages, mostly English, and vocational training while waiting for the result of the procedure to determine their refugees status and resettlement in other countries. Most refugees stayed for one year before being resettled in a third country, but some had to stay for quite a few years. When the camp finally closed for good in 1996, some 6,000 refugees were forced to return home because they were not considered victims of political or religious persecution. Hundreds refused to go back to their homelands and committed suicide instead.

Without the benefits of advanced technology such as the Global Positioning System like we have in the present, we could have had landed back in Vietnam, or in Thailand, Malaysia, Indonesia, or even the Philippines after floating days, weeks, or even months at sea. Where we started out, the South China Sea is like a big bowl of water. To the northwest of the bowl, there is Thailand. To the southwest and the south, lie Malaysia and Indonesia. To the east and northeast, are the islands of the Philippines. There was no doubt that we did not want to return to Vietnam; that would destroy our whole purpose of escaping, plus we would have had to face an unknown, dark future. We had learned that a Thailand refugee camp was overcrowded due to the refugees who traveled by land, and a lot of unwanted situations happened to the freedom seekers who sometimes were robbed, raped, or even killed in the vicinity of the Gulf of Thailand. In regard to the Philippines, the longest distance away, we would have to spend weeks or even months at sea to get there, due to unwanted reasons such as storms. These destinations were not the ones we had in mind. Malaysia and Indonesia were our two most desired countries — getting there would require the shortest time and potentially the least troubles. However, the best scenario for us was, to be rescued, after a day or two, by a foreign ship — not a Vietnamese or Russian one, we hoped — in international waters. This would eliminate all potential dangers that awaited us every single second we were sailing on our little boat.

DAY 2

Life Goes On

A huge wave rocked the boat and knocked the toolbox over, spilling all its contents onto the floorboards in the engine cabin, producing sharp, clattering noises that woke my sisters and me at the same time. All three of us, lying supine on the wooden floor with eyes wide opened, tried to fast forward through all the events since we'd left home. Raw, painful memories were still lingering, as our beloved father was still lying right next to us. He seemed to be sleeping rather than dead. After recovering from all the emotions, all the shedding of tears, I finally had a chance to look at my father up close. This was the first time I had really looked at someone in my family for a long time without awkwardness. So many memories — mostly good ones — involving with my father went through my mind in a flash; but I quickly realized that things were never going to be the same without him alive. At home I would never sit still, watching my loved ones sleeping. It would probably have been considered rude to do so.

Generally, Vietnamese people did not express our love for each other in public. We did not hold hands in public. We did not hug in public. We did not kiss in public. We did not say "I love you" in public. We just did not act certain ways in front of other people. However, that did not mean we did not love each other or care for each other. It was just something we were all accustomed to while growing up, without any questions. As a matter of fact, I did not even see a husband and a wife hugging each other in front of me once. Such scenarios would be considered lascivious displays in public. Older adults did not want to set "bad" examples for the kids; and younger couples did not want elders to

51

criticize their "misbehaviors." Teenagers sometimes had boyfriends and girlfriends, but usually they had to keep their relationship a secret to the point where their best friends might not even know. Parents certainly did not want their kids dating while they were in grade school. For the most part, people would display behaviors not for their own benefit, but for others to see. Therefore, everybody — young and old — had to watch their own backs while doing their acceptable *and* unacceptable things. The worst thing that could happen to a person was for people say bad things about him or her. Nobody wanted to be in that kind of situation. We were probably one of the few peoples in the world that were still very old-fashioned about the expression of our affection. But the majority of these show-no-affection-for-each-other people still got married, had many kids, and lived happily with each other for a long, long time.

Marriages were especially old-fashioned among the rural families. For the most part, young adults were free to choose their potential mates. However, their parents usually had the last say in their knot-tying. They used several criteria to determine their children's future companions. Those criteria mainly had to do how well the two families would fit together. In short, people built marital relationships based on social status. Financially, the two families had to be on the same level; the parents did not like their son or daughter to marry someone from a poorer family. And people with college degrees would not likely marry someone without a formal higher education. This went hand-in-hand with the family's finance, since only wealthy people would be able to afford their children's costly education. Parents also wanted their kids to marry someone with the same religious faith. This was especially the case with Christians — mainly Catholics. In almost all cases, the other party had to become a Christian before the marriage could take place. Sadly, sometimes couples could not unite due to their origins in terms of locality. In Vietnam, we had three regions: the North, the Central, and the South. People from each regions had a very distinctive accent and a slightly different dialect, which were not welcomed by some families of different regions. When it came to marriages, Vietnamese people could be very prejudiced. However, all these discriminating-selection processes may very well provide couples with the least differences in their religious, economic, and social lives, which may allow them to have a fuller, happier, and longer marriage.

Throughout the night, while I was asleep, my two brothers had been outside taking turns steering the boat. At this moment, I could tell the engine was running strong at full throttle. I was lying there listening to the slapping of the waves onto our boat and the splashing of seawater from both sides. Out of curiosity, I sat up and looked, through the windows at the expanse of water and sky. My heart was filled with awe instantly when my eyes met the massive waves of the sea. My body trembled as I got on my knees and put my face up close to the opening to witness what seemed impossible. I was like a kid who went to a circus for the very first time and had a chance to stand next to a colossal elephant; a kid who had known, that an elephant was big but could not comprehend just how big until he stood next to one. With amazement, my jaw dropped; my eyes bulged to a point that, if measured, would have landed my name in *Guinness World Records*. These humongous swells gave me an illusion of riding on the world's biggest roller coaster track. But maybe roller coaster tracks could not be this big. A better description would be those hilly roads of open, mountainous country where it takes a car a minute or so to reach the foot of the hill and requires a longer time to reach the top. Once when we were at the lowest part of the swells, I felt like I was on a dry seafloor between two massive walls of water that would collapse and bury us deep in the bottom of the sea. When at the top of the swells, I felt like I was on top of a mountain overlooking the surrounding valleys. At this time, looking through the windows, I could only see the crests of the next couple of waves and no foot of any distant waves was visible, except for the one our boat was about to fall into. We were in an up-and-down motion as if our boat was a big fishing bobber floating on huge waves, which all resembled one another, giving me a feeling that our boat was not even moving at all. What was definitely moving was the bilge water that rushed over the ribs of the boat toward the stern when our boat headed for the top of a swell and it went the other way when she headed down the slope.

My two brothers were wearing translucent plastic bags, serving as raincoats. I could see that their hair — even with caps — was flat and droopy due to wetness. Their bare, wrinkled hands and feet looked like they had been in the water for a long time. The greater light could not yet penetrate through the extremely thick low-flying clouds, which contributed to the misty rain, yielding a very low visibility. The air

was so saturated with fine particles of water that those standing outside would be soaking wet in no time. That was the case with my two
brothers; it was as if they were standing underneath a patio with a
water-mist system.

Even sitting inside the hull, I felt the dampness of my clothes as
if they just had been pulled straight out of the washing machine after
the final spin. Not just our clothes, everything else on the boat was
damp from the misty rain. I did not know whether it had any effect
or not, but breathing in this moisture from the air did not make me
feel thirsty at all. That helped since drinking any water would induce
vomiting because our sick stomachs just could not take anything.

Seeing us awake, Tuan came in and told us that he had no idea
how long we would be on the boat, and therefore we had to put our
father into the water. Instantly he was met with my two sisters' vis-
ceral oppositions. "*Khong duoc! Hay de Ba tren tau,*" they pleaded,
entreating him to keep our father on board. Their instantaneous objection to my brother's statement were like lightning, as if their minds
had already been made up a long time ago. And then my two sisters
started to scream. In the process, they stretched out their arms like a
soccer goalie in such a protective way that they dared Tuan to touch
our father. My spinning head was clear enough to think far ahead.
After seeing and hearing the emotional response from my sisters, it
made sense to me that we should keep our father onboard regardless
of what uncertainties we were going to face. As a tradition, we valued
our loved ones' death anniversaries more than any other important,
personal dates, more than birthdays, baptisms, first communions,
confirmations, graduations, or wedding anniversaries. We would spend
more money on a funeral for a deceased family member than on any
other personal events. At home, our father would have all ceremonies
performed on his body as the Temple of God, before he would be placed
into his final resting place, a cemetery — a holy land, behind our church,
as we thought of it — reserved only for local Catholic members. All relatives — near and far — and probably the whole town would come to
pay their last respects. Back in the village, I even went to the funeral
to offer my prayers for someone that I hardly knew; it was just the
right thing to do as I was raised. As for our father, we would visit his
grave whenever we wanted to, but for sure all family members definitely
would be at his graveside on his death anniversary to pray for his soul,

in addition to reflecting on and celebrating his life. We loved our father so much that it was natural that my sisters did not want to let him go just like that. Once we let him go, that was it. He was the main reason why we were sitting on the boat searching for freedom. He was the one who always wished to bring better lives to all of his children. However, his wish had not yet been fulfilled at this moment. We had no clue what was going to happen later, but for now nobody was leaving the group. We left Vietnam together as a family. We were going to sail on together as a family.

Tuan crawled back outside, conversed with Tu, at the helm for a quick minute, then came back in and told my sisters that we were going to leave our father on the boat. There was a sigh of relief among us three. I could tell that there was a smile under the stern face of both of my brothers. I believed that they wanted to do the right thing. They wanted to behave like mature, strong-minded men, leaders of the family who could not reveal any emotion at any time. I was sure that my two brothers did not even want to proceed with the previous plan, and wanted their younger siblings to make that decision. They threw it out in the open so that their decision would get full support from everybody. At the same time, their manhood would not be tarnished. Our beloved father was the father of all of us, so nobody had the right to settle the matter alone. I was glad that the decision had total blessings from everybody.

Tuan asked my sisters and me to help him wrap up our father in our only blanket, which now was damp and cold due to the humidity and the misty rain. People said that a corpse always felt heavier than when that person was still alive. I knew this to be true when four of us tried to pick our father up so that we could slide the blanket underneath him. Our father probably weighed about 120 pounds but, strangely, we could not pick him up together on a count of three. Could it be that the myth about a person weighing more dead than alive was true? But all of us were deeply emotional knowingly that this could be the last time we were ever going to see our father's face. We had been without food and water for more than twenty-four hours, and had been thrown up everything that we had consumed before the escape, and our bodies were exhausted. And we could not even kneel without bumping our heads. Together these things made it difficult for us to physically lift our father.

After all the commotion, we were able to wrap our father neatly and secure the two ends with small ropes to keep the blanket from unrolling; we carried him a couple of yards away from our sleeping area toward the front where we were keeping the supplies. We placed him on the right-hand side of the storage area with his head pointing toward the bow. That was the last time I saw our father's face, the face of the man who I wanted to emulate. I grew up wishing that one day I would turn out just like him. I was so overwhelmed with my loss that tears started to flow down my cheeks as fast as water dripping from a badly leaking faucet. I just let my nose run because I did not want to make any sniffling noises revealing my emotion at the time. I heard my two sisters' uncontrollable weeping. Still, these cries seemed to be minute compared to others I'd heard mourning and grieving their loved ones at home. Some went as far as hiring criers who did all the pitiful and sorrowful shrieks for family members who could not do such thing in public at their loved one's funeral. People — especially the young and women — had to shed tears at a loved one's funerals; it would not be right if they could not do this. They sometimes needed one person to start the commotion and the rest certainly would follow, since emotion could be very contagious. Other people were watching their moves so they had to act appropriately. Tuan acted much like any other big brother whose actions serve as a role model for younger siblings. His facial expression showed neither sadness nor happiness. He moved swiftly as if there was nothing holding him back. His tired eyes were bloodshot but I could tell that he was determined to pick up the baton and finish the race that our father had started. Likewise, Tu, while at the helm, had a stern-looking face that only aimed straight ahead. His glossy eyes were fixed onto the continuity of the oncoming waves. Not a single time during the whole ordeal would he glance at what we were doing to our father. He was physically and mentally the toughest of the bunch and he certainly looked it. Life-goes-on and nothing-can-stop-me attitudes truly defined his stubborn personality. He was the reason why we went on sailing instead of returning back home. For a million years, I could never act like my big brothers. I could not see much of anything anymore, so I wiped my watery eyes with the sleeves of my shirt and tried to take deep breaths to ease some pain. My breathing was interrupted and cut short several times due to the incredible emotion. His life was too short, I thought. There was so much future in front of him. He had wanted to deliver his children from the dangers of the sea to the lands of the free, and he was stopped short of doing that. And danger still could strike us at any moment.

We had tasted our first shock and awe of the sea when we had reached the open water from the calm water of the rivers. After our father died, we surely weathered the greatest storm of our lives. Many things went spiralling south, just like we'd gone under the water and felt suffocated, struggling to surface with air was nowhere to be found. The physical bombardment of the water slapping against our boat, the mental feelings of the loss of our beloved father, the uncertain future, and the sense of danger had all taken away our appetite. None of us had eaten or drunk anything on the boat.

In the engine compartment, we had a round kerosene stove hanging by three ropes that were dangling from a nail embedded onto the wooden ceiling of the cabin. By hanging the stove, small movements of the boat would not knock the pot over. The current seas were not rattling our boat severely; she traveled up and down the repeated swells and troughs without any difficulty. It made sense perfectly when I glanced over and saw Tuan who was tending the fire on the stove with some steam coming from a cooking pot, though I had never seen him cook at home. After a sniff of a beautifully familiar aroma I knew that he was cooking rice. However, I was so exhausted that I fell back asleep next to my sisters.

I was in a deep sleep as if I had been operated on and was still under anesthesia. "*Tai, ngoi day an com,*" said Tuan, telling me to sit up to eat. Tuan touched my chest and rocked me a little bit with his right hand. I slowly opened my eyes to the sight of a small bowl of plain steamed rice in my brother's hand. I sat up and received the rice bowl with a choice of fish sauce or soy sauce in two small shakers sitting on the floorboard right next to me. In addition, a plastic food container had some fried, dried, salted fish in it. My mother had prepared this fish and it would stay good for weeks without refrigeration. I noticed my two sisters still lying there and asked Tuan that whether they had eaten anything. He told me that they were too tired and did not want to get up to eat. I thought that as a fine young man I should be physically better than my sisters; therefore, I was going to eat. After I said my prayers, I began to eat the rice with my hand. I do not know why I did that, since that was not normally how I ate; I used a spoon at home. I did not like to use chopsticks as my parents did, because I was clumsy with them and I was always afraid that my siblings would eat all the food before I could eat my share. My brothers always said that I should eat less than them since I was smaller than them. I always thought that they were teasing me and never believed them. I kept on eating more and faster than everyone else in the family. It seemed like I had to fight for every single grain of rice every single day.

Our saying was that every grain of rice was a drop of sweat or a tear of a farmer; therefore, we should not waste any at all. People believed it was a sin to do so. When we finished eating our bowls should not have any trace of food left behind. If there were some leftovers present, our pets would do the honor. Ironically, while eating we had to avoid making noticeable contact noises between the utensils and the bowls, because such noises would indicate empty bowls said to be signs of how broke we were going to be. Nobody wanted to be broke and hungry, naturally.

Even though I did not feel hungry at all after almost two days without food, I still tried to eat, just to make my brother happy and at the same time not to waste any food. When I swallowed my first bite, my dry throat hurt so much that tears came from my eyes. The rice was a little uncooked and dry; it probably had needed more water and cooking time. For cultural reasons, not many men would go into kitchens. They generally worked outside, which would explain why mothers — usually homemakers — were always the best cooks in the family. However, I did not care how bad the rice tasted at this point. I truly believed that I had to eat to stay alive, so I grabbed some more rice and stuffed it into my mouth. This was worse than the time I had to eat tofu every day for a couple of weeks straight. As I began chewing on it, I coughed and started to throw up. It happened so fast that I did not have time to grab a bucket or a sick bag. As a normal reaction, I covered my mouth with the palm of my hand while looking around, but the pressurizing force was so enormous that vomit exploded through the crack of my lips. My vomit was all over me. Some of them again landed on my sleeping sisters. First the food I had just eaten came out. Then food I had eaten two days earlier came out. Finally yellowish fluid came out. It was so strong, fast, and sudden that I felt like my intestines were coming out at the same time. To compound the awful feeling of undigested food flying out of my mouth, my nose was full of rice. It was so forceful that I even felt some food might have flown out of my ears and eyes. I became disoriented for a moment as I tried to unplug my nose while my watery eyes became blurry and my ears deaf. Everything in front of me seemed to be far away and all noises had faded into silence. My whole body hurt so much that I collapsed face-down on my own vomit. I coughed so hard and at the same time tried to catch my breath with my mouth drooling. Tuan saw the whole thing, came over, and rubbed my back to ease some of my pain. It helped.

After a few minutes of heavy breathing, I regained some of my senses and began to sit up straight. I grabbed a cloth nearby and cleaned myself up with it. I then proceeded to wipe off the floorboards with it, but the cloth's absorbance had its limit, therefore I was smearing the mess rather than picking it up. As it turned out, the old cloth was the engine rag; its oiliness gave me the camouflaged look of a U.S. Marine.

Since I could not eat any rice, Tuan thought I should drink some water and chew on a cube of brown sugar to get some energy. This made sense so I hastily agreed. But it was another bad choice. As soon as I took a few sips of water from a plastic cup and had a bite of a crunchy cube of brown sugar, I immediately went into vomiting mode again. It was the worst physical feeling that I ever felt; I thought I was going to die from it. The good thing was that I had not heard of anybody dying from throwing up. I lay facedown, sobbing, and warded my brother off, "*Di ra di.*" I childishly thought that my brother was trying to kill me, so I vowed not to eat or drink anything from him again.

Darkness came. There was no lesser light. There were no heavenly bodies. However, there were sparks, emitted chemically from the splashing of the waves, which simultaneously produced a limelight similar to the millions of fireflies that were rampant in our village during those hot, humid, dark summer nights. I used to catch a whole bunch of these lighted beetles, kept them in a glass jar, placed the jar in a dark room, and used it as a nightlight. If I caught a good number of them, I could actually read under the light generated by these critters. It was so interesting that these living creatures had this ability. During courtship they produced an intermittent light from luminescent chemicals in their abdominal organs. Unfortunately, these poor captives never survived the next day to give me another show.

The wind began to howl a little louder. Occasionally, it channeled through the windows at a right angle, producing the longest whistle, one that no human being could possibly make. The waves slapped against the boat, stronger and stronger. Tonight was the second night we were at sea, but I had begun to notice that the water was a lot more turbulent during the night than during the day. It seemed that God and His angels were patrolling and calming the sea during the day. The devils seemed to be out there roughing up the water surface at night, trying to disturb our faith along the way. The water surface was not pitch-black like the night before; with millions of chemical sparks, it appeared gray with white, refulgent foaming at the edges of the crashing waves.

As the night went on, the wind picked up, the distance between the wave crests became shorter, and the height of the waves became taller. The boat was no longer able to roller-coaster on top of the waves, but now had to spear through them. My brothers had a hard time breaking these waves while trying to stay on course at the same time. Because they constantly had to watch out for dangerous waves, when they looked at the compass after several consecutive hits, they were off course by some tens of degrees. For every attempt to correct our course, our little boat had to pay dearly to the crashing waters. For every single wave we broke there was a loud boom that followed; then, immediately, the wood of the boat creaked. My heart began to pound like a bass drum as if I were waiting in anticipation for something that was about to happen. Would the boat stay intact? For every single time there was a collision and nothing happened disastrously, the merciful God surely had blessed us. As the rough weather continued we need seventy-times-seven blessings to stay afloat. Occasionally, we encountered waves that had a strong back wind pushed against them, creating high, stiff drop-offs. These unfriendly waves caused our boat to nose-dive into the water, but miraculously we surfaced every single time.

The area my sisters and I occupied was covered by some sheet metal that had come from some old sheds; hence they had a whole bunch of nail holes which looked like heavenly bodies on those nights with a bright lesser light while I slept inside. We had a few minor water leaks when it rained. However, when the boat went for a nosedive, sea-water crashed over the deck like turgid water streaming down the street after a broken levee. First, the water came down from the rooftop in strings of beads as if we were under a heavy rainstorm. Then, it gushed in from the two portholes as if people were standing outside with buckets of water, dousing. To make matters worse, the bilge water was agitated from the rocking motion of the boat and flew at us hard from underneath. I felt like we were sitting inside a large dishwasher that had pressurized water squirting from all directions. Under these circumstances, my sisters and I were constantly under unwanted showers. And we were cold. This condition was so much like times I had spent in the river for hours, throwing mud and water at other boys. I had so much fun then that I failed to notice that my skin had turned into that of a Caucasian. However this time was no fun. The old tires hanging on the front and on the sides kept slapping our boat after each crashing wave, so my brothers just cut them all loose. This helped. Later in the evening they let our fishnet go too, because it was too bulky. As our boat rolled, the two ends of our fishnet had kept getting into the water, affecting our boat's stability. Getting rid of the net helped during the turbulent seas, but we were sad to lose an item of survival gear.

Our boat started getting heavy due to the rise of the bilge water. The bilge water pump had not been working since our father's accident. Throughout the night, my two brothers had been taking turns going down to the engine cabin to draw up bilge water by hand. Currently both of them were occupied with the critical sailing of our boat. Tu told me to go down to the engine compartment to draw up the water by using the bucket made from an old vinyl-composite, military-police helmet. The helmet had an attached rounded wooden stick serving as the handle. It was so sturdy that after many years of use, it only showed a little wear and tear. Our boat had a wooden box attached onto the inside wall of the engine cabin. Here where bilge water was mostly concentrated since it was the lowest part of the boat. The box had a small hole on the outside wall of the boat at the bottom edge of the box that could channel all water in the box to the outside by gravitation. So I stood on one of the ribs of the boat in a stance like a sumo wrestler's, with my left hand on the wooden box and my right on the helmet bucket. This spot was a very small section of the engine cabin where we could squeeze in to crank up the engine by hand. There was a lever on top of the diesel engine that when lifted up caused the engine to have no compression at all. Pointing that lever straight up was what we had to do when we tried to hand crank the motor. When the face of the person doing the cranking turned red, he would flip the lever to a horizontal position, which activated the compression, causing the first cylinder ignition to fire. He then hoped that the momentum he had in the heavy flywheel would cause the engine to keep on firing; otherwise, a second round of cranking would rob all his breath. One time after I had the engine started, the crank handle slipped out of the socket and whacked me hard on my bare left shin. I screamed so loud that I felt as if the boat started to vibrate, creating a ripple around our boat. I learned a valuable lesson from the incident — that I had to spread my legs wider while cranking the motor. I also needed to lift my face up so the crank handle would not crack my jaws. Getting struck on the face by a steel crank handle could be a lot worse than getting punched by a professional boxer, and surely would yield major surgical facial and orthodontist work.

While drawing up the bilge water, I had to be very careful not to touch the hot running engine. This chore was not as simple as it looked. It required hand, foot, and eye coordination to obtain good results. I was barefoot, standing on the greasy, slippery floor of the boat, drawing up buckets of water that seemed to weigh at least a hundred pounds each. I stopped to rest frequently because I felt so exhausted and nauseous. My head was spinning as I tried to remain conscious to perform my duty. I did not feel so bad when I was lying down. Every hard blow of a wave to the side of the boat, I lost my balance, fell down, and gave myself a bath. I got up every single time and kept drawing the water thinking that my two brothers were trying hard up there to keep the boat afloat. I got numerous scrapes and burns from falling and touching the hot engine. It hurt but I tried hard to hold back my tears, as my two sisters at this moment were offering prayers continuously and diligently *"Kinh mung Ma-ri-a day on phuc Duc Chua Troi o cung Ba ..."* ("Hail Mary, full of grace, the Lord is with thee..."). We were on this together; everybody had an important role to play. Mine was to empty the extra weight that could pose problems. My physical strength had diminished a long time ago. What was left of me was mental stamina, the knowledge that I had a role in this fight for survival. Unfortunately, my ability was no match for Mother Nature as the outflow of seawater appeared to be overwhelmed by the inflow. When I first started hauling up the water, the bilge water's level was about at my ankles, but the level now had crept up to almost half way up my calves.

It was very discouraging but I was thinking to myself that I could not give up. I steadily drew up one helmet at a time. We all were in it together to get through this hard time.

The devils really went on a rampage as the night went on. The sea became more turbulent, and the collisions between the boat and the water got more violent. Sometimes a wave lifted up the nose of the boat and on the way down we encountered another wave that produced a loud boom causing her to shake fiercely. It felt like she was breaking apart after each collision. "How many more times can our boat get hit like this and stay in one piece?" was a question that remained in the back of my mind. With each strong wave hit, as I was performing my duty, I heard the creaking of wooden boards. I was thinking that our boat structure must have come loose somewhere to produce such a sound. She was flexing her limit and that was not a good sign. On top of that, she had been built three years before and had never been tested under this kind of powerful stress. The quality of the materials and the construction of the vessel were both unknown. We did not know how much abusing force she would be able to absorb. Occasionally, a back-chasing wave lifted up the stern of the boat and then all of a sudden it disappeared, causing our boat to free-fall. The result was that the back deck was immersed in seawater, which in turn poured its contents mercilessly into our engine cabin. As winds produced more unpredictable waves, it became evident that my brothers were having a harder time trying to keep our boat on course. The combination of the heights of the waves, wavelengths, and the length of our boat had a devastating effect. It did not matter what direction we sailed, eventually we would collide hard by one of the rogue waves.

It seemed that humans versus nature would end up with a winner and a loser. Constantly bombarded with the relentless waves, for sure, our untested wooden boat would certainly end up on the losing end at some point. Nothing in this world is ultimately be able to withstand the forces of Mother Nature. It did not matter how hard my brothers tried or how skillful they were, their efforts were so futile against their nemesis. Having constantly negative results along with irrational thoughts in their minds, my brothers were galvanized to try something different and they hoped that it would give them different results. That was to shut off the engine and let the boat floating free at the will of the wind and the ocean current until rough water calmed.

Their illogical decision seemed to be the right one at the time. The whole night we had been cutting against the grain of the wood. Now we changed our cutting angle and the outcome was as different as day and night. The boat now was floating alongside the raging waves. She was now mostly touched and slightly rocked by these forces of nature. There were a few times that we got scared, when the boat was out of position and got rocked hard by one of those rogue waves, but the results were not anything like a while back when we had been constantly subjected to the violence of the sea. This relatively gentle sailing offered all of us peace of mind. Our prayers had been answered by our Father in Heaven and my two sisters, comforted were able to stop praying and lie down to fall asleep.

I was still slowly drawing up bilge water with whatever energy I had left in my body. However, now I was able to make headway slowly. The bilge water finally retreated, leaving two oily, black rings around my legs. And Tu came in to relieve me of my duty. I handed him the bucket and I thanked the Lord, knowing that I could not have continued on any longer. Wet, filthy, and smelly from the bilge water, I crawled up to the sleeping area to join my sleeping sisters. My hands and feet were all wrinkled like those of a little kid who loves the water so much that he does not want to leave the bathtub until his veins turned black and his lips purple. I was not alone; we were all wet and cold, and we did not have any dry clothes to slip into. I am not sure if dry clothes would have made a difference at the time, since water continued to bombard us constantly. Maybe a wet suit would have been helpful. I hit the floor right next to my sisters and fell asleep immediately, I was so tired.

DAY 3

Ship Sightings

For the rest of the night, my brothers took turns staying up to keep watch and empty the bilge water. While one was dutifully awake, the other went to sleep to replenish his tired body to weather the next obstacles. We had been floating free for five or six hours before strong winds subsided. It happened right before daybreak when all of the devils seemingly vanished and their horrible works disappeared with them. When I first opened my eyes, my brothers had started the engine and put our boat back on course to continue our journey; daylight was upon us. Again the air was filled with fine mist; visibility was very poor. The air had so much water in it that it was like sailing in a very thick fog, something with which we were very unfamiliar. The greater light could not break through the mist to reach the surface of the sea. Even if there had been lands filled with vegetation and fruit trees near us, with the low visibility we would not have been able to spot them. The best light we received from the greater light was not even as bright as the light inside a fluorescent-lit office building. The crashing waves were long gone, leaving only huge swells which allowed us to sail on top of the water surface like we were riding a roller coaster once more. We did not mind this condition, because it was easy on the boat and on all of us at the same time. In the meantime, we were truly sailing under angels' wings. There had been so much going on during the previous two days and nights that made this moment unique in terms of composure and reflection. Our beloved father had been taken away from us without any warning. My brother's decision to keep going had been made despite all the potential risks and uncertainties. Keeping our father on the boat did give us a feeling of his constant presence among the five of us. Bad weather the night before could signify many more bad storms — possibly worse ones — we were going to face. That was why at that moment we were truly sailing without any worries. After so many hours of rough sailing, the relatively not-so-rough sea was a blessing. Mentally awake, I was lying there with my eyes closed, savoring every second, and hoping that the rest of the journey we would only encounter this relative ease.

We were fortunate to enjoy this kiddie roller-coaster ride for a few more hours without any incidents. Suddenly, Tuan shouted, "*Co tau kia! Co tau kia!*" ("There's a ship! There's a ship!") I jumped up from my horizontal position and nearly shaved my scalp against the cabin ceiling. In the engine compartment, emptying out the bilge water, Tu swiftly rushed outside. I followed him to join Tuan on the back outboard. Tuan pointed his finger straight ahead, showing us the first ship we'd seen since we left the coast of Vietnam. I had to give my brother a lot of credit for spotting the vessel, since it was only vaguely visible to the naked eye through the misty air. I faintly saw a cargo ship, but it quickly went out of sight as our boat hit the foot of a swell. As our boat rose to the top of the wave, the ship reappeared. Rightfully excited, Tuan had already changed course to chase after this potential lifesaver. Even though it was probably tens of miles away from us, this vessel appeared to be sailing from our right to our left. Our father was right about our schedule, that between two and three days of sailing, we would be able to see foreign vessels, since we were in the international waters. Many "boat people" had been saved in this vicinity by ships. Without a doubt, this ship sighting made us feel very good about ourselves, because as a group we had accomplished something. Perhaps we might be rescued.

Tu grabbed a stick with a soiled white shirt at the end, which he prepared earlier, and started to wave furiously to draw attention. In this current type of weather, a red or an orange shirt might have worked better than a white one. A flare fired into the sky or some kind of electrical distress- signal producer would do a thousand times better than what Tu was doing. However, we did not have that kind of luxury onboard. Without binoculars, the cargo ship still looked huge, even at a great distance away. We were not able to see any crew members, but there must have been hundreds of large crates stacked next to and atop each other.

Our father knew that our boat might be too small to be noticed on the vast sea. He had prepared a metal bucket with chunks of tire rubber, pieces of old rags, and fuel inside to produce an S.O.S. signal. Once we saw any ship, we needed immediately to light the contents of the bucket. The fire would give out a lot of black smoke, making us more noticeable. Once we were seen, we would be rescued. Plans were that simple. Tu handed me the stick and told me to keep waving. With one hand on the boat's mast, I waved the makeshift flag energetically, hoping my effort would catch someone's attention. I was thinking that if someone on this giant ship spotted us — our little fishing boat — it would stop and rescue us immediately. Hope of being rescued filled up in my mind, and my heartbeat raced up as fast as that of a hummingbird. I held my breath for a longest time, as if any exhalation would shatter all hope that I accumulated for the previous three days.

After removing the lid from the oiled-rag bucket, with a box of matchsticks in his hands, Tu proceeded to light up the rags. He repeatedly struck a matchstick against the coated side of the box as if he was a Stone Age man trying to make a fire from two flints. The tiny wooden matchsticks kept breaking. He kept sliding open the box to grab another one until he clumsily spilled the whole box all over the back deck. He grunted repeatedly in frustration and grabbed indiscriminately for one that would give him light. Light was what he wanted at this moment, but it was so hard to get. He went through almost ten matches before he finally got a fire started. The fire gave us an instant sigh of relief. We were in business, sending out our distress signal. A large, dark column of black smoke rose quickly into the atmosphere. A combination of fuel and black rubber really did a good job of revealing our presence. We eagerly awaited rescue since we must have been spotted by the ship. There was no way that people would miss that much black smoke in an otherwise empty sky. While waving the flag and looking on, I did not realize that I was doing some skillful tap dancing. By this time, I started to see more of the back end of the ship. I believed that Tuan was going at full speed. Still, he kept grunting and pulling the throttle cable as if he could not believe that he had gotten all the power from the engine, which roared at its maximum capability. Our little boat was going so fast; had she been equipped with wings, she would be ready for take-off right now. Probably a few miles of separation were as close as we would be to that ship. A minute later, all we saw was the whole back of the ship. The ship kept getting smaller and smaller until we could not see it anymore in the misty air. I can't remember when I stopped waving the flag, but when I came to my senses, the flag was lying on the deck and I was hugging the mast with both of my arms. At the same time, I could not recall when I stopped dancing. Tu started beating himself on the chest and blaming everybody for not doing enough to be noticed. Maybe what we did was not good enough for my hot-tempered brother, but I thought we did what we could to get attention. Unfortunately, good results had not prevailed. I felt like we had been robbed, beaten, and left for dead by the robbers. That a stranger had happened to walk by then, but kept on walking without offering any help. I sobbed with despair. Those people on the ship probably did not notice our existence, still I felt neglected and abandoned. We had missed our opportunity to be rescued. The sea had an enormous area. We were like a grain of sand in the middle of the Sahara. Chances were that we would not get this kind of opportunity often.

Tuan eased up on the gas and he seemed to be confused about what he needed to do next. My brothers began exchanging intense words that were derived from their shattered hope and disarray. Tu blamed his brother for not paying close enough attention to spot the ship sooner, so we could have more time to go after it. Tuan blamed his brother for not lighting up the signal bucket soon enough. A spat escalated to the degree that I could envision a devil referee standing between the two, wishfully encouraging a brawl. I could see that they were furious enough and ready to choke each other to death. My two sisters intensified their cries, making our boat look like an accident scene where two drivers were blaming each other with their kids crying in the background. It was so chaotic that I could see that there was no end. Fortunately, I was wrong. With our loving God's help, Tuan began to back down from the senseless confrontation. At the same time, Tu held back his harsh voice toward his brother. They both seemingly had finished delivering all their differences and realized that they were going nowhere with hostility. I believe this had a lot to do with what kind of environment we were raised in. While growing up, we never saw our parents argue in front of us; and they never taught us right from wrong by yelling at us. Tuan and Tu had all this in their heads unconsciously. The first step of facing reality was to get our boat back on course. Our first goal was still trying to be rescued by one of the foreign ships with humanitarian souls onboard. The second goal was to reach land as safely and quickly as possible, because the longer we were on water, the more danger we were likely going to face. Tuan slowly changed our coordinates back to 120 degrees southeast and again put the engine on full throttle. From this time on, we really stayed alert for other ships. Still looking furiously, Tu murmured something to himself while putting the lid back onto the smoke stack to extinguish it.

It was probably a couple of hours past midday, but the sunlight could not quite spear through the decks of cloud and the thick, misty air. As I was standing outside, beads of water dripped down from my droopy hair due to so much moisture in the air. The air was as warm and wet as the air inside a steam room. The temperature was uncomfortable but I did not feel thirsty at all, because I felt like I could probably sip the water right out of the air. We usually faced this type of weather during our raining season; therefore, it did not bother us much as we were trying to spot another foreign ship. We just could not afford missing any chance of being rescued. Tu took over the control of our boat and pushily demanded that Tuan and I watch out for other ships. I knew that my bumptious brother — a self-proclaimed leader — did that because he had the worst eyesight among the three of us. That meant that Tuan and I had to cover a lookout scope of 360 degrees. The visibility was very bad; my health was on the decline; and my vision was at its worst ever. I could not see that far anymore. While staring at the blank sea, I did not blink my eyes much, because I was afraid that in a split second another ship might appear and disappear. We just could not afford missing out again. Sitting near the stern of the boat, I looked to my left for a while then turned to my right for some kind of sign. After a couple of hours of looking tiredly into empty spaces at waves that all resembled one another, discouraged and somnolent, I asked Tu permission to go inside for a break. He did not say anything as if he did not hear me talking. I went inside anyway and lay down next to my sleeping sisters. Throughout the rest of the day, I was in and out of the cabin frequently to keep my hope alive. For hours, Tuan sat in one spot near the middle of the boat, right on top of where we slept, to scan for another ship. Filled with patience and a positive attitude, he believed that he would see the next one very soon, and he would not let it get away this time. He was wrong. Both of my brothers were outside the boat all day, but they could not see anything. It was just us and the water.

Darkness of night again smothered us. My brothers huddled at the command center with the map in front of them. Tuan, using his index finger, drew an imaginary circle and gave his co captain the estimate of our current location. By looking at the legends on the corner of the map, I was sure he was completely correct, because the circle he drew had a radius of at least a hundred miles. Tu had no objection because he knew for a fact that we were in the middle of somewhere and that somewhere was in the South China Sea.

The devils had started getting busy again as the wind began to pick up strength. We knew right away that we would be sailing into another storm again. The misty air was no longer there as if the wind had pushed it somewhere else after the disappearance of daylight. Our bodies were now cold and dry from the wind. Our clothes had become stiff from the salt of the sea. There were many times that we got wet, air-dried, and then got wet again. I figured there was no need to change, since we would be wet again in no time. In addition, we probably did not have any dry clothes by now.

As the wind was blowing, we felt so hungry and dehydrated, but anything we ate or drank our bodies just rejected. We still tried. However, every time we swallowed some food, my two sisters and I never failed to vomit so hard that we collapsed, grasping for air. After three days of trying, we just felt a lot better by not eating or drinking at all. I would have enough justification for not eating and drinking when I remembered how bad I felt while I threw up. My dry lips cracked like a windshield catching a foul ball. When I stuck out my tongue to wet them, I did not know whether the salty taste came from seawater or from my own blood. Layers and layers of white film, natural salts, flaked off my skin like I was a snake in the midst of molting. My naked legs were full of chalky chicken scratches. I looked like I was in the desert rather than in the middle of the sea.

Toward the middle of the night, the hissing sound of the wind became more noticeable. Mother Nature wanted to test our boat again. This storm was so similar to the one we had confronted the night before. Our boat had to break one wave after another to move forward. The more resistance we had, the more powerfully the crashing waves hit our little boat. She was slapped around so much that my brothers — having learned from the night before — once again shut down the engine and let her sail with the wind and the current. Shutting down the engine was not what we'd wanted to do, but it was the most effective way to minimize the potential damage our boat might receive from confronting those relentless waves. We were now sitting inside a floating bobber that the wind and sea current could carry it wherever they pleased. Our boat still rolled constantly but the severity was negligible. There was no argument that shutting down the engine was again the right choice. On this night we had decided to do this a lot earlier than the night before. The quick decision gave us a feeling of being in more control of our situation. Likewise, stress and anxiety were lower, even though catastrophe could strike at any time. Like the night before, we had no idea where the wind and current would take us. Nevertheless, between two choices, we had to go with a safer choice. We did not need to be scholars to figure it out that we were in a better shape now than when the engine was running. My two brothers were outside observing and monitoring the situation, as our little wanderer was totally at the mercy of the breaking waves and the multidirectional winds.

As the night went on, the devils did not give up their horrific works but increased their intensity. Wide awake from turbulence and completely filled with the fear of going under, my sisters and I broke out our prayers again, asking the merciful God to spare our lives and to deliver us from evil. Our prayers — supposedly to be carried out with undivided attention — were interrupted many times because powerful waves constantly rocked our boat. Seawater flew in from the portholes as if firefighters were standing outside aiming at us with powerful water hoses. We had to grab with both hands onto parts of the boat to keep us from falling from our seats. After those violent collisions, our faith wavered. We stopped praying. We screamed our lungs out, thinking the boat was about to sink. We were deathly frightened. At that instant, our little faith shattered and the devils had temporarily succeeded. Thankfully, with the grace of God, we did not go under when momentarily we had become lost sheep. However, the loving God did not abandon His children, and He gave us the strength to regain our composure and faithfully continue our prayers. The devils had so many chances to conquer us, but the Holy Spirit was omnipresent to prevent such a downfall. The three of us continued with the rosary as the devils bombarded our carrier from all directions.

Tuan and Tu took turns going into the engine compartment and drawing up the water to the outside. Keeping the bilge water low was essential to our survival. The lighter the boat, the better she would stay afloat. When she rolled, bilge water rushed to one side of the boat. The more bilge water there was the higher degree the boat would roll. All heavy things such as the engine, the transmission, the fuel drum, and the freshwater containers were situated in the lowest part of the boat; ultimately, such a design gave our boat a low center of gravity. Once she rolled, this low center of gravity would pull her back to an upright position. Too much bilge water could prevent this, though, because if it outweighed other things combined, the boat could never return to her original position once rolled, and doom would be inevitable. My brothers did a good job of emptying out that water when it needed doing. The wind did not seem to slow down a bit; we did not know where it came from and where it would be going, but it blew steadily and hard throughout the night.

Tired but awake, my sisters and I kept our prayers going strong, asking the merciful God to send His guarding angels down to protect our lives and our fragile little boat. The whistle of the wind, the rocking of our boat, and the repetition of Hail Mary composed a lullaby that affected my concentration. Dead tired, at some point, I faltered and fell to sleep. My two exhausted but persistent sisters remained faithful with their continuing prayers. They did not wake me up; instead, the pitch and roll of the boat brought me back to a state of alertness. I did not know whether I moved my lips or not while napping like I used to do when we had our family evening prayers at home, but when Ly saw me opening my eyes, she softly asked, "*Tai sao khong thuc de cau nguyen?*" ("Why aren't you awake to pray?") I did not answer her but carried on the prayers with my sisters. A moment later, I had my eyes closed up again. Waking up after having my head banging against the side of the boat, I saw Ly looking at me in the eyes and she asked, "*Tai sao khong thuc de cau nguyen?*" Again, I went back continuing on praying with them. This time, the boat took a hard nosedive that threw me off my seat and jolted me awake, again from being half asleep. I shamefully looked at Ly who once more time reminded me, "*Tai sao khong thuc de cau nguyen?*" I did not and could not answer her but I kept on praying with them until all three of us dozed off into oblivion. We all must have felt at peace, because all of us fell deeply asleep. We were out completely. People can buy almost anything, but there is one thing people absolutely cannot buy, and that is peace of mind. Peace of mind has to be earned, somehow we were blessed with it while the everlasting wind kept roughing up the sea, which in turn pounded our little floating wanderer mercilessly. The three of us were able to sleep through it all.

A few hours before daybreak, Tu urgently rushed into the engine compartment. He yelled loudly, "*Co tau kia!*" while pulling on Tuan's arm. It was Tuan's turn to take a breather in the engine room while Tu was outside doing the lookout, while our boat was still free floating. Tu had spotted a ship, and just like that, we all were up. Tu swiftly grabbed our flickering hurricane lantern hanging inside the engine cabin and crawled back outside. After grabbing the flashlight, Tuan was half a step behind.

A short distance away, some lights illuminated a whole corner of the dark sea. The lights were moving our direction with a very good velocity. Within seconds, they were close enough to our boat to reveal their identity — lights on an ocean liner. With this second ship sighting, we were so happy, and hope of being rescued by this ship started to ring loudly in our ears. Chances were that this ships would pick us up and either take us all the way to another country, giving us a new home, transporting us safely to one of the refugee camps, or giving us food, water, and fuel, and showing us how to get to the closest refugee camp. To us, seeing a ship this close made it seem that the loving God had sent one of His angels down to rescue us. All these positive visions started to build up in our minds as this vessel quickly approached our location. It was like we had been lost in a thick and tall forest, with no idea of getting out, when suddenly a team of rescuers appeared out of the ruggedness, spotted us, and took us to safety. Excitement built up to a max in every one of us. We had come this close to the ship, we ought to be rescued, we thought.

Standing on top of the engine cabin, with one hand on the shade cover of the helm operator to maintain balance, Tu waved the lantern from side to side, with the other hand signaling to the approaching ship. Tuan switched on the flashlight and hoped that the high-intensity beam would catch attention from people on the vessel. But his hope immediately vanished when the flashlight failed to light. He banged it a couple of times on the deck and it still did not produce a light. He quickly uncapped its battery compartment to check its condition. As it turned out, the battery casing and the batteries were full of rust caused by high salt concentration of the seawater. He let out a roar that sounded like the one coming from the king of the jungle. In the process, he spiked both the damaged flashlight and the corroded batteries onto the deck. His hands now were covered with white powder from the batteries. He stood up, stared at the approaching ship, and could only hope for something good to unfold.

Tu's exultant face soon looked worried, as if he sensed impending doom. He waved his lantern at a faster pace and at the same time emptied his lungs, as if the people on the ship would hear his pleading. Tuan was still standing there petrified as if his hands and feet were tied and his eyes blindfolded. Our boat was floating parallel to the waves; as soon as I got up, I peeked through the right porthole and saw this ship coming straight at us. It did not seem to slow a bit and seemed likely on a collision course with us. With a huge steel vessel and our little wooden boat, we all knew which one was going to be in trouble. My sisters and I, helplessly sitting inside, saw this ship coming and quickly did a sign of the cross on our foreheads. We clasped our hands, bowed our heads, and started praying individually. I cannot remember exactly how I prayed. However, during these critical seconds, I probably murmured like this: "*Chua Gie-su, xin cuu chung con. Chua Gie-su, xin cuu chung con. Chua Gie-su, xin cuu chung con,*" calling upon Jesus to save us.

Not giving up his focus, Tu was still working hard at his lantern-waving, down to the final seconds. Even though his face had been filled with anxiety, he remained hopeful of being seen. An untimely breaking wave splashed directly onto the right side of the boat knocking my sisters and me, praying, off our seats. The roll of the boat brought Tu to his knees but he still managed to keep his arm up with the lantern above his head. He was like a boxer with a big heart who stubbornly refused to stay down. The big splash fanned out with thousands of watery arms, with each arm letting out thousands of water droplets. They flew through the windows and gave the three of us a shower while we were on top of each other. Exactly one devilish water droplet must have had a heat-seeking missile flying directly at the lantern's globe.

And then a high-pitched pop was clearly heard. A big hole was carved out of the glass globe, which immediately shattered into countless little pieces right in front of Tu's stunned face. Before he could realize he had a broken globe, a sinister breath of wind quickly blew out the wick—leaving our whole boat in total darkness. Holding the extinguished lantern, he looked at the oncoming ship as if he was a timorous deer standing in the middle of a mountainous road and staring at the headlights of an approaching car. The whole incident was like a precise concert of destruction. It happened methodically, as if there had been a devil standing right next to Tu, who broke the lamp and extinguished the fire so that we would not be seen by the oncoming ship. "*Chua oi!*" ("My lord!") roared Tu in desperation. His facial expression now contained neither hope nor anxiety; it was filled with fear—fear of not being seen, fear of getting capsized by the oncoming ship, and ultimately fear of dying in the water.

At the same time, a great roll caused the petrified Tuan to lose balance and hit the deck with his whole body. The hard fall snapped him back to the reality, in time for him to shout loudly to us to get out of the boat, "*Ra khoi tau, le len!*" In darkness, with water still dripping down from my face, I grabbed a life vest and hurriedly clambered to the outside via the engine cabin. I felt like I was crawling in one of those trenches and foxholes behind our school's classrooms. The only thing different now was that I was not carrying a wooden rifle and throwing wooden grenades as the battle exercise called for when Vietnam was at war in Cambodia and with China. For a split second I foolishly thought I was floating alone in the water. We'd had a hard time on the boat; how were we going to stay alive in the water? I believed that this huge indestructible ship was about to crash into our little fragile boat, and thought that I needed to get out fast, to jump into the water before the collision. I did not want to be inside when that happened because our boat wreckage definitely would pin me in. My two sisters were right behind me grabbing my ankles.

Halfway through the engine cabin, with all the negativity going on in my baffled head and all the chaos happening to the five of us, my hands and knees slipped and I fell flat on my stomach after another huge roll of the boat. With all my energy from the awkward horizontal position, I plunged forward, passing the cabin door like a football running back trying to cross the goal line while being grabbed by a bunch of tacklers. With a cluster of scrapes, I managed to get outside in time to stare at the huge oncoming block of steel. Our boat was like a little squid that was about to be gulped down by this giant whale. At that moment, things happened so fast that we did not even have a moment to think what action would be best for our survival. We were stunned. We were frozen. Nobody was giving out any direction. For sure, staying on the boat, our lives had been hanging on the needle thread at all times. What chance would we have if we were floating on the water with only a life vest? Without water, without food, without protection from the elements, and without visibility to be rescued by foreign ships, how long would we be able to survive? That did not even include consideration of all the aggressive creatures of the sea. Even though with many dire thoughts flying around and the monstrous giant approaching fast, no one was ready to jump into the raging water. It seemed innate and logical to us that by staying with the boat, we would have the best chance to survive. A minute ago, excitement of being rescued prematurely circled our thoughts. Now those excited thoughts turned into hopes of not being tragically crushed. Our lives were hanging on a balance and they certainly could go either way. If this moving giant missed us, we would live to continue our journey. If it collided with us, the result would be death.

With ten unblinking eyes glued on this approaching monster, we prayed for our lives that this beast had spotted us. At the same time, we could not envision the boat wreckage that we were going to face if we had not been seen. It was like sitting in a malfunctioning airplane falling nose-first from the sky; deaths were imminent, as we stared at the ground, which was getting closer and closer. Being children of God, breaking out a Hail Mary could have been the most appropriate thing right then, but we did not. For a few seconds, our fierce stares were lit by internal infernos — and reflected the steel mammoth that was about to run us over. We had exhausted our human efforts and we just stood there facing the destiny that God was about to cast upon us. We had done what we could. We physically had no more control at this moment. Certainly there was not enough time to jump into the engine cabin, start up the motor, and get away from this trap.

As the steel giant was about to cast its shadow over us, it responded — like a driver waking up in time to swerve back into the right lane — surely the merciful God's plan, gradually turning to its right. From my inner being, I seemingly heard the iron squeak as if this whale of steel had physically twisted its rigid body to change its forward momentum. Before we realized its new bearing and its direct effect on our survival, the bow of the ship went by us. We looked up as if we were looking at the top floor of a five-story building. The first thing that caught my wide-open eyes was the huge ship anchor, which was probably bigger than our boat. As this titanic machine sailed by us, it looked a lot slower than when it approached us directly. With our mouths wide open in astonishment, we silently looked at this great wall of steel inching past. We seemed to be waiting for something to happen, as if we were sitting uneasily in a movie theater staring at a blank screen, waiting for the first graphic to pop up. However, nothing was about to flash on the big screen.

The vessel was brightly lit, but we could not see a single human being. It looked more like a ghost ship than anything else. Then we all shouted and yelled for help. Somehow, we all started at the same time, as if there was somebody standing there counting to three for us to start the synchronized commotion. Tu with one hand grasping the boat mast, desperately reached out with his other hand, trying to grab onto some part of the ship. He closed his eyes and held up his fingers as if he was feeling the steel of the ship's body. It was so close that if I were somebody in those Chinese kung fu movies, I could have leaped aboard the ship. We stood there letting out the most deafening screams a human could possibly produce, trying to get somebody's attention. Nothing happened, though, except for the ship slipping away. If I had been strong enough, now would have been the right time for me to sling our boat anchor toward the stern of that goliath. With some luck, the anchor would hook onto the rail, the ship would drag us behind, and we would probably be saved in no time. Unfortunately, it went by us, giving our boat its wake, just like a passing vehicle giving a hitch-hiker a disgraceful splash of the water from a muddy puddle. Rhythmically bobbing waves were the only tangible thing we received from this vessel.

We were fortunate to survive this debacle. The ship must have been cruising slowly, otherwise, it would not have been able to change course in time to avoid a collision. In addition, the water pulled by its monstrous propeller would have sucked us right from the water surface, and we might have vanished without a trace as those vanishing vessels in the Bermuda Triangle. It was so close. I watched the rounded stern of the ship disappearing from sight. My dry throat hurt so badly — from the screaming, like I had swallowed a razor blade, and I started to break down in tears as my latest hope of being rescued faded away fast. I was devastated as I hopelessly crouched, my face buried in the palms of my hands. I could not stand the look of the disappearing ship. I just wanted to pause and capture that image of the ship in front of me, so I would not feel alone on the sea anymore. My sisters were even more in disarray than I was. Both of them threw themselves onto the deck and drummed on it with their fists, like little kids throwing tantrums. It looked like nobody was going to come over and picked them up and comforted them like used to happen at home.

That was as close as we got to the ship, but Tu—fierce warrior as he was — would not let it be gone so easily. He immediately jumped into the engine cabin and cranked up the motor while Tuan took control of our boat and put her on full throttle to chase after this evanescent vessel. Presumably, crews on the ship did not see us; rationally, we had to go after them. Right on its tail, we were sailing against the most powerful rushing water generated by this ship's gigantic propeller as if we were on a kayak trying to paddle against a strong current upstream. We zigzagged uncontrollably within a huge stretch of bubbling waters. It seemed like it took a whole day for us to drift from the ship's front to its end, but now the vessel appeared to sail away from us with supersonic speed. It was as if they were running away from us as fast as they could. Our boat's speed was no match for the colossus, and it was gone from us without a trace within minutes. Unfolding in front of our eyes things involving our potential deaths had happened quickly, but in our minds this poignant event seemed to happen in a slow motion, an agonizing torture that imprinted a deep scar in our long-term memory. The immediate feeling of being neglected and ignored was overwhelming among us five. Not being rescued could be as venomous as the bite of a rattlesnake. What had happened to us was the opposite of all the feel-good stories from other "boat people" who were seen and rescued by so many foreign ships. We were right there, but we were not that fortunate. How close could we get and what could we do to be rescued? My two sisters and I broke down crying like lost children who had been abandoned by their parents in the middle of nowhere. As for whether my two strong-minded brothers wept, I did not see it, but I believed they did it silently and secretly, not wanting anybody or even themselves to see and know.

My sisters had cried so much that they were losing their voices. One could never tell that they were crying with a lot of emotion. However, deep down, they were two of the most passionate people I had known in my life. They would sit and sob the whole time while watching a sad movie. Whenever the main character faced tragedy, they became emotional; unfortunately, this time they were the protagonists. That made this unfortunate situation thousands of times worse than every sad movie they had watched. And I was no better. Again, I felt like we had been robbed, beaten, and left for dead. During the day, a first stranger had walked by and left us there untouched. Now the second stranger happened to pass by and looked, but did not offer any help. This was not what I had envisioned about our journey. Our father had told us that we would be rescued if we were spotted, at least that was part of the plans but it did not work the way our father had envisioned. I was raised in a family where if I saw a person falling to the ground, I would rush over to help. If I saw a blind person trying to cross the street, I would dash over to offer my set of good eyes. If I saw a destitute person, I would stop and give a couple of coins. Seeing somebody who needed help, my parents would help. Therefore, it was hard for me to digest horrible thing that had just happened to us. I was sure there were millions of reasons why people would not stop to make a rescue. Nevertheless, what was more important than to save a human life?

In November 1985, Captain Jeon Je Yong of a South Korean fishing boat called Kwang Myung 87, came within a hundred yards from an overcrowded boat with ninety-six Vietnamese "boat people" onboard, that had been trying to be rescued in international waters for days, while stranded due to a mechanical failure. On his way home from Singapore, after temporarily stopping his ship, the captain, age forty-four, radioed his superior, asking permission to rescue these helpless people. Many of these people were old, or very young, and some were pregnant. Jeon Je Yong's ship was one of at least twenty ships that these "boat people" had seen in a wandering week, but no ship had stopped to help them, as if they were invisible on the sea. The captain's request to pick up these poor people was denied. As a result they were seemingly left alone again. About half an hour later, by the grace of God, another ship came and rescued these people. As it turned out, this ship was the same one captained by Jeon Je Yong that had left them. After leaving those people, the captain had checked the weather forecast and learned that there would be a big storm coming. He believed that the troubled boat would not be able to withstand the coming force of Mother Nature, and he decided to turn around and rescue them. A huge storm did come and stir up the surface of the sea, but ninety-six lives were saved. A few days later, while still sailing on the sea, the captain was given an order to get rid of those people by any means, which included putting them on a makeshift raft. Again, he refused to follow his superior's ruthless order. He kept them on his ship until he arrived safely in Pusan, South Korea, and handed them over to the South Korean authorities. Within a year, every single one of these "boat people" was granted asylum by the United States and Canada. As for the unforgettable hero in the eyes of many Vietnamese refugees, Captain Jeon Je Yong, who directly saved almost a hundred lives, got a pink slip for insubordination.

As the heartless ship disappeared into dark empty space and its lights were gone completely, Tuan gave up his pursuit. He idled the motor, put the gear on neutral, and sat down dejectedly on the edge of the boat. He looked confused and kept shaking his head. An overwhelming feeling of lassitude prevented him raising his head. He could not accept the fact that we had been right there and done all we could, but we still had not gotten any help. Nobody could say that we did not do enough on our end. An answer was out there but we failed to find it.

Meanwhile, Tu sat down with his back against the mast of the boat, clearly depressed. This was the first time I had seen such disappointment in him. If one could cry in one's heart, Tu had that kind of look. He was always vivacious and during our escape I had not seen him sleep once or take a respite. This unfortunate event surely had taken a great toll on him. Now he was just sitting there quietly and staring blankly out to sea. I did not know what he was thinking. However, he looked like a losing pitcher who had allowed tie-breaking home run with two outs in the bottom of the ninth. Lucky for us, Tu had never been a quitter. We just hoped he would not become one now. After some quiet time, he surely would get up, with his indefatigable spirit.

"*Chua Gie-su oi, xin giup chung con*" ("Our Lord, Jesus, please help us"), mumbled Ly with her face buried in the palms of her hands.

Strangely, the forces of nature immediately eased, as if the vanished ship had scooped up the storm with it. The wind subsided noticeably and the rough waves seemingly retreated to a bearable condition. Then sprinkles suddenly turned to torrential rain, as if the loving God was shedding tears over His abandoned children, forcing my sisters and me to go inside for cover. Unfortunately, being inside did not help much. Water came through holes, cracks, and other openings, so that we seemed to be under a miniature shower. What did probably help was protection from the wind outside. Somehow, this shower did wonders for all of us. It was like a chill breaker, a wake-up call, and a cleanser that washed away all our bad memories, alleviated our anxiety as well as our pain, and allowed us to start anew. We could feel that there was a new flow of vigor that completely energized our bodies and souls, as if we had been baptized in this shower and reborn.

As my sisters and I were sheltered inside, and after my two brothers got their senses back thanks to the tears of Mother Nature, we were ready to continue with our journey. Tuan put the rope, his security belt, back around his waist, not having realized that he'd had it off for that whole frightening time when we'd nearly collided with the ship. As a nonswimmer without a life vest in the dark, raging water, he could have been submerged instantly had he fallen overboard. With all of the chaos, that he did not slip and fall out of the boat was truly remarkable. One of the guardian angels protecting our little boat must have personally tucked Tuan under his wings.

After regaining their equanimity, my brothers again huddled at the command center to look at the compass, as Tuan shifted the gear to sail at the former bearing of 120 degrees southeast. As I looked at them, they did not show even the slightest discouragement at all. In fact, they were full of enthusiasm and ready for the next challenge, as if they were excellent football cornerbacks who a minute ago had gotten burned for a long touchdown, but now moved on to prove their worthiness. They knew that they *had* to move on in order to save our lives.

DAY 4

The Flood

The floodgates of heaven had been fully opened; water came down hard continuously. Looking out of the portholes, even with just a faint trace of light, I could tell that the raindrops were falling perpendicularly, creating huge floating bubbles as they hit the sea. I had been told that whenever I saw bubbles produced by raindrops on the water surface, there would be a lengthy rainstorm. That proved to be true this time. Without strong winds, the wavelengths started to stretch out further. There were very few breaking waves. The surrounding water was relatively calm and quiet except for the beating of raindrops against the sheet metal above our heads. My brothers kept taking turns going down to the engine cabin to draw out the bilge water, which was filling the boat fast, as the rain continued. We stayed on course under this wet but calm condition until morning. My two sisters and I again were able to fall into a body-rejuvenating sleep, even though the rain kept falling on our heads — literally.

When we saw the first tinge of light from the sun marking the beginning of a new day, there were only light sprinkles present, and very little wind. It seemed like the rain had sent everything in the air down into the sea. We had not seen these calm conditions since day one. After a few hours of rest, my sisters and I felt much better, since the sea surface was relatively gentle. We began to feel a little hungry. We might have been able to eat some solid food. However, we had learned it the hard way during the last few days, so we were not inclined to touch it at this time. Fortunately, with hours of gentle sailing, we managed to sip some plain water to keep ourselves hydrated. I drank some water just to make my caring brothers happy even though I did not feel thirsty at all due to all of the water I had swallowed from the rain.

A few hours after the first daylight, visibility got better but the greater light remained hidden behind decks of clouds and misty air. My sisters remained still. There was no reason for me to get up; therefore, I was just lying there with eyes closed while thinking about all those horrible things that had happened to us and wondering what was going to happen to us next. Then I heard my brother. "*Ca heo kia!*" ("There're dolphins!") exclaimed Tuan excitedly. I got on my knees, looked out of our left aperture, and saw a stir of the calm sea. Suddenly, a huge, dark-gray and pearl-white image jumped out of the water. Then another one followed, astonishingly. They would have cleared the height of our boat by a good margin had they jumped over us. I had seen them in movies and books but never seen them in person before. This was the very first time I had actually seen live dolphins and they appeared only a few yards away from my ecstatic eyes. My sisters were also up now and looked through the right porthole. It sounded as though they were also enjoying the show these dolphins were performing. I was afraid of missing what my sisters were seeing so I crowded my head between theirs and we all watched the same show on the right side. There were twice as many dolphins on this side of the boat. There have been at least twenty of them. Some were repeatedly jumping out of the water as if to make their presence more obvious. The rest swam gracefully and playfully along our boat as if challenging us to a speed race. It seemed like these dolphins knew exactly how excited we were and they seemed to enjoy showing off their flipping and jumping ability. Their beautiful and flawless performance was the best show on earth. I believed that these natural actors could easily have outperformed any of those trained captives in amusement parks.

Watching those amazing dolphins play brought a smile to Tu's face for the first time since we'd been at sea. His broad smile looked as natural as it could be. He could not stop smiling, as if he did not have any lingering bad memories and anxieties. As for Tuan, nothing could stop his excitement. He jumped up and down like a little kid attending an animal circus for the first time in his life, quiet no more. He kept going and going, and I didn't even know what he was talking about, as if he were talking baby talk. The only thing I knew for sure was that he was very happy at this moment. Seeing the gregarious dolphins play, not only allowed us to witness nature at its finest, it also delivered a great welcoming sign for our journey. Culturally, whales and dolphins were the Vietnamese fisher's best friends. There were tales about how they had carried drowning victims to shore. Survivors recalled how these mammals swam underneath their troubled boats to support them during violent storms. Some fishermen went so far as naming whales and dolphins their patron saints. Biblically, a big fish swallowed Jonah and released him alive after three days. For such reasons, whenever there were dead ones washed ashore, the locals — presumably the fishers — always tried to bury them. Besides humans, they were the only creatures that received a burial in Vietnam. That said a lot about the respect people had for whales and dolphins since as a people they would otherwise consume any animals they could find.

The dolphins were indeed a great boon since the whole day went by smoothly without any incidents. The wind blew gently and steadily all day, creating huge swells that all looked alike. We repeatedly traveled up and down, tracing a gigantic sine wave. Sailing without any worries, we would have loved to see dolphins again in the near future. In such a comforting situation, my sisters and I slept most of the time. While my brothers took care of the operation of the boat, they still did not forget to sweep the sea for another ship. They were not going to give up hope of seeing another one. While one was taking care of business, the other one took a nap. They switched their roles every four hours or so.

Before it got dark, I could see the transformation of thick, white clouds into dark, gloomy ones on the horizon. These threatening clouds slowly crept our direction. They seemed more than ready to dump all their contents onto our little floater. The wind started to reveal its presence again, too. As an effect, the sea swelled up. The boat started rocking and I got nauseous and started throwing up again — possibly all the water that I had drunk earlier. The boat was rocking from side to side as we sailed into the night. Rainstorms became inevitable. Water again poured down like there was a big showerhead on top of us and somebody was playing with it.

Having learned from the previous two nights, my brothers immediately shut down the engine to minimize the wave impact. They felt very good while doing that, believing that they had gotten everything under control. However, our conditions worsened with the motor off. Winds seemed to come from different directions, creating irregular, crashing waves that were neither huge nor small. They hit our left side; they hit our right side; they hit our front; they hit our back. Sometimes they hit all four at the same time. After half an hour or so of this extreme turbulence, my brothers became weary and started the engine to break through those unavoidable crashing waves and run away from others instead of letting the boat float free like the two previous nights. Most waves were of a particular size and if we broke them at a certain angle, there would be much less impact on our boat. In addition, my brothers had to adjust the speed of the boat so that it would be in sync with the height and the length of the waves, as we were trying to ride the waves as much as we could. Unfortunately, when storms like this occurred, waves' size, shape, and form became unpredictably irregular and they frequently and violently knocked us around, but my brothers maintained their calm to guide our boat away from potential catastrophe. Having the engine running did give them a lot more control over our situation. Therefore, the decision was made to keep our boat running through this bad weather; we just hoped and prayed that our decision was the right one that would give us another safe night.

A few hours into the darkness, the waters were still a little rough, but the boat seemed to be all right and my brothers apparently had everything under control. The boat was on course according to plans. However, the main reason for this was not due to the experience they had gained over the previous nights; the fact was that the storm did not get any worse as the night went on. We had to be thankful for that. But rain kept steadily pounding our small vessel. We did not have even a little dry spot for refuge. Still, the rough and wet conditions did not deter my sisters and I from sleeping.

Well into the night, Tu shook us urgently while we were half asleep. "*Thuc day! Thuc day!*" ("Wake up! Wake up!") He then commanded us to put on our life vests, which were stuffed with crushed Styrofoam, tailored by our father. Putting on our life vests became necessary whenever crisis arose, so I hastily complied without questions, even though I did not know what kind of emergency we had at hand. My two sisters slept with their life vests on — despite the discomfort. In his hand, Tu had our globe-less hurricane lantern, with the wick up really high, which produced a huge flame spitting out a pillar of black smoke. This had been painting graffiti on the underside of the rooftop with its soot, wherever it moved. Under the light given off by the lantern, I could tell that we were not in a good situation; our boat was a pool of water. Every time we hit a wave head-on, there seemed to be a powerful energy that transferred through the walls of the boat and created tidal waves right inside it. Boxes, jugs, pots, pans, and other articles floated around, bumping against each other, producing a raucous mix of disturbing and haunting noises. Among those floating items came our poor father — still wrapped in the blanket — gradually moving away in the rising bilge water. Suspended in water, the old army blanket wrapping our father had swelled up to twice its original size.

As soon as our father died, a decomposition process immediately began. This process is called autolysis, or self-digestion, and involves the breakdown of complex protein and carbohydrate molecules into simpler compounds. Then putrefaction would have begun. This is the destruction of the soft tissues of the body by the action of bacteria, fungi, and protozoa. This process internally produces gases such as hydrogen sulfide, methane, ammonia, and sulfur dioxide, especially in the bowels, causing an inflation of the abdomen. After four days, our father was probably at this stage, which surely caused his body to float in the water.

While securing my life vest, I looked over into the engine compartment where I saw Tu who had hung the lantern on a nail right above the running engine; he was emptying the bilge water to the outside through the wooden box at an expeditious pace. Even under the shifty faint light of the kerosene lantern, I could see beads of sparkling sweat trickling down from his forehead. He also breathed in and out heavily, which probably indicated how long he'd been at his current task. When I finished strapping on the vest, he handed me his bucket and told me to take over his duty while he would go looking for the source of the water leak. Now, I knew exactly what kind of problem we had on hands. We had a *leak*! I just hoped that the damage was repairable; otherwise, we would be facing big trouble in no time. My brothers usually did everything by themselves, but by asking for my help they definitely revealed the severity of the situation. Having had no food for the previous four days, I did not have any energy. I even had a hard time lifting my arms. However, once I saw the water and after I heard

Tu's command, a burst of energy helped me up on my feet and I started energetically bucketing out the water. I did not know where I had gotten my energy from, but my life being threatened probably had something to do with it.

The duty of emptying out the bilge water was like a relay race; Tu had passed me the baton and now it was up to me to finish the distance. Still, at my current pace, I was not getting the bilge water out fast enough because the water level was now approaching my kneecaps as I stood on one of the ribs of our boat's structure. Almost half of the boat was filled with seawater! At this time, the rising water began to touch part of the flywheel of our diesel engine, causing the water to splash all over the cabin. The sprayed water got onto our engine's non-insulated exhaust pipe that immediately produced hot steam, just like in saunas of the rich and famous. Water coming out of the spinning flywheel hit the cabin walls and ceiling at a high velocity, splashing water in every direction, like going through a car wash. Besides being wet, my body was covered with engine oil, mud, vomit, and everything else in the water. I wiped my face with my hand constantly and kept turning my face to avoid the water jets, so I could perform my duty — this slowed me significantly. At times, I momentarily stopped to clear debris from my eyes, which seemed now not to be keen as they had been. As a matter of fact, I started to see doubles of everything. More often than I could count, I slipped on the greasy ribs of our boat and fell down with my legs pointing straight into the air, resulting in more unwanted baths. I kept biting my lips and getting up more and more slowly every time I was down. I felt like a hurting boxer who needed almost a full ten count before he could stand. Each bucket of water seemed to weigh a ton to me. And I definitely wasn't keeping pace. The bilge water outflow was a lot slower than the inflow of seawater. The water level now had passed my knees. Seawater filled more than half of the boat! My brothers had given me this job to do and I had to do my best. Unfortunately, I kept slipping and falling due to the rocking of the boat. I had a long way to go, but I could not give up.

Seeing the dire situation from the helm, Tuan barked out his disapproval. "*Tai, len day!*" (Tai, get up here!") I dropped the bucket and crawled out of the engine cabin to meet him in the back where big drops of rain were now falling down sparingly. The raindrops seemed as big as golf balls — one that splashed on my face actually hurt. Tuan berated me for not working fast enough and said that we were about to sink. He was that blunt. I was thinking that he should not say that word — "sink" — because it might bring us bad luck. According to some Vietnamese thinking, it is taboo to mention certain negative things. For instance, while flying on an airplane, we just did not talk about the possibility of the plane crashing. When riding in a car, automobile accidents should never be brought up. Walking in the dark, ghosts should never come up in conversation, and for those crossing a river on a small boat, the word "alligator" should not be uttered. That was why at this moment I was surprised to hear Tuan say "sink." As his little brother, I was not supposed to talk back, even if he was wrong, but in this critical situation, he was right. We were sinking. I did not say a word. He stormily demanded that I take over the steering of the boat while he would go down and stay in the engine cabin to do the job that I could not do. The good news was that he picked up the baton I had dropped and so our team might finish the race. The bad news was that he had passed me a different baton for a different race — a more important and difficult race that required strategies, instincts, and lots of luck to reach the finish line. It was not wise to entrust a callow boy with such an important responsibility, but I know that my brother had no other choice at this moment. Since we had left port, I had not touched the tiller handle once. It was as if a football coach, with his team down by two, had sent a third-string kicker out to attempt a fifty-yard field goal with a couple of seconds left on the clock. All odds were stacked against me.

With one quick move, Tuan untied himself. With a few tricks he had learned from being a former boy scout, he then had the same rope securely knotted around my waist. He jerked me around like he was putting a pair of pants on a stubborn, cranky kid. I winced as he surely had cinched the security rope too tight. As painful as it was I, I couldn't complain with critical issues at stake. The other end of the rope was already firmly fixed to the boat to prevent me from being tossed overboard. Shouting into my left ear, Tuan tersely instructed me to look at the compass and to keep the magnetic needle pointing at 120 degrees southeast — a bearing we had been using since the evening of the first day at sea. I also needed to watch out for the side-crashing waves because those were the most dangerous ones that could easily capsize the boat. This meant that I had to sail perpendicularly to the crashing waves as much as I could while maintaining the bearing. Throwing me an earful of succinct instruction in less than ten seconds, Tuan also flooded my ear with rainwater from his lips, then, not even waiting for any questions, he disappeared into the engine cabin.

I parted my legs to get a more stable stance. While holding onto the engine cabin top with my left hand, I firmly gripped the tiller handle with my right. It was hard to keep my eyes open to maintain my vision while seawater, rain water, and the wind kept pounding my wet face. I felt as if I were a sinner, with a large crowd throwing stones at me. Our water-filled boat sat with her decks almost under the water. Every few seconds or so, the boat took a dive after breaking an oncoming wave. There would be a loud boom, followed by the splash of seawater that spread out like two humongous fans from the bow of the boat. The soapy foam that gave me faint visibility within a few long wavelengths against a pitch-black sky, outlined the seawater with a deep gray color.

After a few hard hits, I quickly eyed the compass and found out that my bearing was sixty degrees off. I promptly corrected my steering only to meet a tall, crashing wave that raised the bow of our boat to a seven feet. When the crest of the wave passed half the length of the boat, the bow dropped straight down as if a giant hand had let it go. A loud boom was all I heard and then seawater splattered over both sides of the boat. We were truly blessed because I thought the hard drop would break our little boat into millions of pieces. Our boat could not regain her buoyancy instantly, due to the excessive weight of the bilge water, and immediately she met an ensuing wave. We went under that mountain of water like a submarine diving from the water's surface. Our boat was like a large spear that cut through that thick wall of water without altering its size, shape, and form all in the quick blink of an eye. It was clear that I would be washed away if I did not hang on to the boat securely. I let go the tiller handle and tightly hugged the engine cabin top with both of my hands so I would be able to take the blow of the water hitting my face. There was so much water smothering me that I thought I was having a scuba diving adventure in the darkness of the night instead of standing on a boat. I was afraid that I was going to die.

Meanwhile, my siblings were screaming inside the boat. It was as if they were sitting helplessly inside a closed drum, with somebody pouring water in to drown them. Tuan poked his head out of the engine cabin and let out a displeasured shout, "*Chuyen gi vay?*" ("What's the matter?") Water was dripping down from his body and clothes. I shook my head a few times and avoided eye contact with him. At the same time, I grabbed the tiller handle, looked at the compass, and started acting busy. Since he got nothing out of me, he went back to his duty which was to empty the swimming pool he had under his feet, a pool that was getting deeper and deeper. If not for the two extra wooden boards our father had added to the sides of our boat, we would have gone under by now.

This was the first time I really had a good look at the compass — up close — which was a military type that could flip open like a pocket watch and lie flat on even surfaces. While paying attention to the crashing waves, this time, I slowly moved the tiller handle to get the boat back on the right bearing. She was definitely changing direction, but the needle of the compass seemed unresponsive to small degrees of changes. I then realized that the compass was for use on land. Its needle was not as sensitive during turbulent waters as had it been when on stable ground. I could even tell that the needle was sticking to the glass face, as our boat went rocking through the waves. I kept turning the boat while watching out for rogue waves, as I had been told, until our bearings were roughly correct again. I was sure I was not getting true readings of where we were sailing, but I hoped, surrounded by an enormous sea, that we were heading the right way.

The lives of five people rested in the palm of my hand, depending on me to steer the boat safely. Instead, I almost got us in trouble. At the tiller I felt completely responsible for the well-being of the boat and my siblings. Even though I did not have any control over the weather that could bring catastrophe upon us, I still thought that if we went down, I personally would be culpable. Raindrops kept hammering my face and this was the first time that rainwater actually tasted salty to the tip of my tongue. It must have been partly seawater, since I knew very well that rainwater was supposed to taste pure, unless it came from a polluted sky. A month before our journey, Co Hue, teaching geography, lectured my ninth-grade class about the water cycle in nature. The next day, I was called up to stand next to her table — in front of the class — to deliver an oral report about the subject. She was

delighted and gave me nine points — ten being the highest possible —
for a good delivery. The next day the school principal came, along with
his two associates, and they sat in the back of the classroom to observe
Co Hue's teaching. Before she taught new material, she called several
students up to orally report their home works, the previous day assignment. I was one of them. The subject I had to explain was — to my
surprise — the water cycle in nature again. This time I reported with
real aplomb. I received ten points this time. All the other students
seemed to be doing well with their same questions also. After this oral
exam session, she continued to lecture on the subject she had started
the day before. To us students it looked like she was going over the
same material. We were all so precocious at answering all her questions.
Before the period ended, the credulous trio of administrators walked
out of the classroom totally satisfied as all the students stood up, which
had become our shibboleth, a gesture of showing respect. Co Hue,
who rarely smiled, had a big ear-to-ear grin on her face, and we students felt very good about ourselves for knowing our assignment so
well.

Our boat's decks kept getting closer and closer to the water due
to the water leak. As the winds increased their intensity, the waves
became more frequent and taller. As a result, our weighty boat could
not ride the waves well anymore. While we were sitting low to the sea
surface, those powerful winds scooped up water droplets from crashing waves to create the salty, sideways raindrops that I had just tasted.
As conditions worsened and under stress, I became so weary and nauseous that I began to throw up again in spurts. This was not a good
time to be sick. Since I had not been eating any solid foods for the last
few days, there was nothing in my stomach that could be thrown out.
However, the nauseated feelings were intense, as if my stomach and
every inch of my intestines were tightly twisted to squeeze out whatever contents were left in them. It was like loaded springs were sitting
in back of my throat, compressed to the max and more than ready to
unload through my mouth. I stooped over the roof of the engine cabin,
with my stomach resting against the roof, trying to catch my breath
while still keeping one hand on the tiller. As I was tending to my sickness, I was not even aware of oncoming waves. I was gagging and
coughing, and liquid came out of my ears, my eyes, my nose, and espe-

cially my mouth. Now I was vomiting blood — mixed with thick, yellowish mucous — that plastered all over the compass.

Sounds of the howling wind, raindrops on the sheet metal, splashing of the waves, and breaking of the waters began to fade away from my hearing. Still, I think I heard myself sobbing. I sobbed for the mental and physical beating I was enduring. I sobbed for the personal fight against the unbeatable Mother Nature. I sobbed in the fear that if I failed we would all be going under. However, the main reason I probably sobbed was that I felt self-pity, as a fourteen-year-old boy who had this tremendous life and death responsibility. This responsibility was thrust upon me by default and I was never ready to accept it.

As I became more disoriented from vomiting, I lifted my head and stared at the gray, raging waters. I started to see twinkling heavenly bodies along those crashing waves of the sea. I still slightly heard my brothers who, while shouting frenetically, were still hustling to empty the bilge water and search for the leak inside the engine room. But all these noises and all surrounding objects slowly disappeared from my perception. As my eyelids lowered, the last thing I faintly heard was the ongoing prayers of my faithful sisters, "*Kinh mung Ma-ri-a day on phuc Duc Chua Troi o cung Ba....*" With that, my knees crumbled. My forehead came down — with the force of my body weight — right on the starboard gunwale of the boat, giving me a large gash right above my right eyebrow. Falling down and having one's head bang against something can be serious. However, after my head slammed against the sideboard, I retained consciousness and started perceiving things lucidly if I had been under hypnosis for a few seconds and then had been snapped back to the reality. I felt blood vessels pulsing as blood gushed out and ran down my face, completely covering my right eye. Although the cut was exquisitely painful, it did not hurt my thinking process. My mental acuity had become as sharp as ever. Even with just one uncovered eye, with the sudden rush of adrenaline I unconsciously and quickly stood up and went to regain control of the boat's rudder. Unfortunately, it was too late, as a large rogue wave sideswiped the left side of the boat, tilting it halfway to the right, causing a large flow of seawater to come over from atop the boat's right side rail. My brothers and sisters had another scare for their lives. Chaotic screams from them inside weren't muffled by the howling winds and the crashing waters. And I could tell that some of those screams were aimed at me personally.

At the stern, the deck had been extended backward for about three feet. This extension was enclosed and looked like a big trunk without a lid. On one side there was a small rectangular hole on the floor that we could use to do our private business right onto the water. On the opposite side, there was our additional drinking-water drum, which had been strapped down before we left port. Now the boat's roll was so great that the strap just snapped and the heavy water drum rolled freely. I did not know what I was thinking, but as a natural propensity, I sharply turned around, unconsciously let go the tiller handle, and tried to catch the rolling drum. I could not even touch it, since the short leash — the security rope — stopped me halfway. The drum rolled off the boat right into the dark sea and vanished from my sight. Without hanging on to anything, I was knocked off my feet and fell over the right side. If it had not been for the security rope around my waist, I would have joined the water drum at the bottom of the sea. My bare feet were surfing on seawater, as my underarms hooked the lip of the gunwale. I had never liked unknown waters. When fishing on rivers, occasionally our fishnet had gotten stuck, and I was usually the one who would jump into the chilled, murky waters to free the net. We all knew that there were not any alligators or monsters where we fished, but in the back of my mind there was always one out there that would come and get me. I always got out of the cold waters as soon as I could, with all my body hair standing at attention. As of right now, the water touching my feet felt extremely cold. I felt like there could be hungry jaws below me, aiming for my legs. I shuddered as chills immediately ran down my spine and then split up to reach every single hair follicle of my body.

As my life was hanging in the balance, I did not want to suffer the same fate as our water drum. I would not let go of the boat — not now. I had to get out of the chilled waters *fast*. I immediately cried out for help "*Cuu Em voi! Cuu Em voi! Cuu Em voi!*" Seconds passed. No one came to my rescue. It would be a surprise if anyone could hear my cry, given the pounding of the rain, the howling of the wind, the crash of the water, and the rolling of the boat. At this moment I believed that my siblings were also screaming, also fighting for their own lives. I quickly realized that I was on my own. I had to fight to stay alive; it was that simple. Pull-ups were not my favorite exercise, but they would certainly become handy at this moment. I had my right hand on the rope the left one was on the gunwale; and I grunted like a hog as I attempted to pull myself up. First I got my left leg over the gunwale, touching the deck. Then I slowly rolled, trying to get on deck completely, as the boat rolled to the other side, causing me to fall with my stomach flat on the deck.

While I was gasping for breath in a prone position, Tuan, still with water dripping from his face, poked his head out of the engine cabin again and shouted with an angry tone, "*Chuyen gi vay?*" ("What's the matter?") In spite of the many bombardments, I stood up, wiped the blood off on my face, and took control of the boat's tiller again. Even though I had almost died — from falling into the sea — and there was a big bloody cut on my forehead, I assured him that I was okay. "*Khong co gi!*" I did not want to complicate things since he still had a big job at hand and had no time to listen to my problems. However, I did yell to him that we'd just lost our water drum, our two-month supply of drinking water. I thought he heard me, but I did not see any reaction on his face. Once more he reminded me to be more careful. He then turned and disappeared into the engine cabin where his duty to lay. Losing the water drum was probably a blessing to us, since our boat floated a little better when the few hundreds pounds of water sitting up high was gone from our deck. That was exactly what Tuan was trying to do — get rid of the weight of the bilge water. It was a different kind of water, but losing it certainly served the same purpose. A couple of nights before, my brothers had let go the tires hanging around the boat and our whole fishnet, so we could obtain more stabilization. This time it was seemingly the work of God who helped us jettison the excess weight so our boat would stay float. By the grace of God, I was not part of His jettison plan.

I looked quickly inside the engine cabin and saw, that Tu was working around the running engine where he had removed all wooden floorboards so that he could reach the bilge of the boat. He had started an unremitting search for the source of the water leak from the bow of the boat and was inch-by-inch working his way down to the engine compartment. He hung the globe-less lantern from the cabin roof away from the jets of the water that were still being created by the spinning of the flywheel. Sitting low, with half of his body submerged in the oily bilge water, Tu ran his hands all over the place to look for leaks.

Meanwhile, Tuan was sedulous at emptying out the bilge water.

After that gander, I could have given hustling brother an A for assid-uous action, but an F for his failure at bailing, as the bilge water was now a lot higher than when I had left him the job. But this would not have been fair. I had no idea what kind of damage we had been done. In addition to the leak or leaks, our boat had submerged once and rolled a couple of times — because of my inability at the tiller — caus-ing a large volume of seawater to flow in. If it were me doing Tuan's work, we probably would have gone under by now.

"*Tim ra roi! Tim ra roi!*" Tu shouted in jubilee. He had found the leak! I did not see his face, but from the singing of his voice, it could have been the happiest moment of his life. It was like he was wander-ing in the desert to look for a water source and he found one — not a hallucination but a large oasis. Tuan, with a sigh of relief, laughing with joy, congratulated his partner repeatedly for a job well done. Patting somebody on the back was not something we normally practiced at home. My brothers had worked in public sector and praising some-body's achievement may have been a norm there, but at home my par-ents simply did not pat me on the back for my good work or behavior. They were very chary in handing out praises. When they did, their praises would never be too fulsome; they would only be honest and sincere. They believed that if I were praised or rewarded excessively for things I was supposed to do I would lose the tendency of doing them without reward or lose my humility. Therefore, I would never expect a modicum of praise for any personal accomplishments. I was raised to walk straight, to sit right, to talk respectfully, and to act with pro-priety in public. Whether I turned out to be the good, the bad, or the ugly, it was a reflection of my parents. Most people did not want to be labeled "bad" parents, therefore they would try their best to mold their children so that society would perceive them as being good or at least acceptable. When a kid turned out to be "bad," parents were thought to be guilty of moral turpitude. Every good tree bore good fruit, and a bad tree bore bad fruit. I did not get lectures on how I should act. I only learned how to act through watching my parents as role models. As a result, I normally did not get rewards for behaving the ways my parents behaved.

One time, I was playing with a plastic bow and arrows on the street. An old woman happened to walk by and was struck on the leg with my arrow. Nothing serious. I could have run away with the other boys, but I chose to come over and apologize to this stranger. My good intentions did not mitigate my peccadillo, as this angry person slapped me so hard that I spun like a top before I hit the ground. Sagacious neighbors who saw what happened came to my rescue. The wizened woman hastily walked away without saying a word. Later, my father learned about the whole incident, patted me on the back, and reassured me that I had done the right thing by coming forward and apologizing to the lady. He said that she had the right to reprimand and punish me, but if that he were she, there would have been no slapping. Instead, I would have earned his laudatory remarks for my contrite behavior, showing the intrinsic rectitude of a decent human being after committing a mistake.

At this moment it was appropriate to praise Tu for his job well done. Anyone would have done the same. Without his discovery there could have been disaster for all of us. My two sisters were definitely thrilled hearing the news, and thanked the merciful God repeatedly. To me, the feeling was more than a vicarious joy. It was something ineffable. Tears started to dribble down my cheeks, an indication of how overwhelmed I felt. It was like I was sitting in a run away car that had finally stopped halfway over the rim of a cliff before the whole car plunged down into a bottomless abyss. I was lost, but now I was found. I was dead, but now I was alive.

With a new frame of mind, I devotedly went back to steering the boat away from danger while keeping her on the right bearing. Staying on course was important. There were times when we were off course as much as sixty degrees, but sailing in a wrong direction could be as bad as sailing without a destination. Knowing the source of the water leak seemed to give us extra confidence — and boost our energy — and we were able to work at a faster, more efficient pace. Tuan was no doubt going more quickly at emptying out the bilge water through the wooden box in the engine compartment. And after the leak source was fixed, Tu got himself another water bucket and helped by dumping out the unwanted water through the oval windows of the engine room. They were both sprinting as if they were competing against each other to see which one would rightfully claim a prestigious title — "Iron Man." It was like they were trapped in a caved-in tunnel. They had to claw their way out through the dirt. When they saw a small ray of light, a sign of life, beaming through the darkness, they hustled at digging through that wall of dirt to get to the other side. The result was welcome: the boat slowly regained her buoyancy. She was not that big. It did not take long to fill her and it certainly and fortunately did not take that long to empty her.

As I found out, Tu had pinpointed the leak around the running engine. When he had been running his hands around the engine area to look for the source of the leak, God remembered us, and sent a wind over the waters, creating a huge wave that tilted our troubled boat and knocked my brother over. That same roll of the boat had cost us our water drum and almost ended my life. To Tu, at first, the incident reminded him of the accident four days ago when our father lost his life. However, this time, instead of being caught up in the propeller like our father, my brother's bare hand touched the engine. He was burned badly and withdrew his hand instantly. For the past five years, Tu had worked in and around many combustion engines, and received many burns and other injuries when working with them. This time, the burn he received from touching the engine was more than a regular burn; it contained an important, cryptic message, one that only experienced mechanics could detect. The message was that unusual heat was radiating from a super-hot engine block. An engine temperature gauge would have been able to tell us its condition, but this engine was so primitive that it did not have one. Tu's mechanical instinct was the temperature gauge that directed him to the engine cooling system which profoundly affected our engine's operating temperature. With a quick search, he put his hands on a loose water hose that was filling our boat with seawater! This rubber hose was supposed to deliver seawater to cool off the hot-running combustion motor. The culprit was a double whammy. The engine had not been getting any coolant and our boat was getting full of water.

Our engine did not have a built-in radiator nor a water-pump impeller to circulate the water to cool itself. Instead it had a metal funnel, which was welded onto the rudder blade. When the boat's propeller turned, water was forced into that funnel. A rubber hose connected to the funnel directed the pressurized water into the hot engine to cool it. After the cool water absorbed the heat, it was then squirted to the outside of the boat. The design was simple; as long as the boat was moving, the engine would be able to get rid of its thermal waste. Unfortunately, after many hours of operation, in addition to the rocking of the boat, the clamp that secured the water hose to the engine failed, causing the hose to come loose. We did not know when that had happened but the rubber hose had been filling our boat with seawater ever since. It was so elementary, but would have deadly if it had not been found in time.

That this "accident" happened to Tu was fortuitous. It was a God-sent message delivered to him during our gravest seconds. If it had been Tuan who had been burned by the hot engine, there was no way that he could have perceived what Tu had. I had gotten burned a lot of times when I was down there drawing out the water, but I could not receive any message from those burns. Tu was chosen to receive this message of salvation and hope. In addition to that, his God-given indomitable spirit and wisdom had shed a light upon him that led him to the right area to find the problem. It took a while to find, but at least it did not require a long time to fix. If it had been structural damage, as my brothers first suspected, I can not imagine how devastating the outcome might have been. Again, the loving God had blessed us.

The floodgate immediately closed as the leak was detected and promptly fixed. Our boat seemingly became more stable. I mentally felt a lot better while standing and navigating our boat. The good news gave me new hope, hope of staying alive to continue our journey. The waters and the winds spearing my face did not seem to rattle my confidence anymore. By constant exposure to the elements, I became inured to the hardships of bad weather; Suddenly I felt impervious, and not bothered by obstacles. My whole body and clothes were completely wet but I felt a lot warmer than moments ago. This was the first time that I felt I was completely in control of our boat. This was something for me to be excited about. I was no longer shaken by the size of the waves, the strength of the winds, or the heavy rainfall. As a boy, I had been metamorphosed into a young man, knowing that what I did could have a profound effect on my siblings and me. With God's will, I had been tried, learned, refused to let this boat sink, just like my two brothers who diligently searched and fixed the water leak that could have turned calamitous if it had not been found in time, and my two sisters who faithfully maintained their prayers during the whole ordeal.

Success usually entails a great amount of strenuous work. That was what my two brothers did to empty out all of the bilge water by hand. They emerged from the cabin and told me to get some rest, after our boat had returned to her normal state. Meanwhile my brothers would continue to fight the devils of the sea. I believe I got that special treatment only because I was younger. Seeing that our boat had already regained her full buoyancy, I freed myself from the rope without questions and gave it to Tuan who immediately wrapped a couple of turns around his waist and knotted the rope securely. With all of my God-given ability, I had successfully accomplished the impossible mission that had been thrust upon me. My brothers had handed me the baton to finish the race. They had entrusted me to kick that end-of-game field goal. And I'd *made* it. With the grace of the omnipresent God, we worked together harmoniously to escape the work of the devils. The will of God will always prevail and it certainly was revealed through our determination. After the ordeal, I had a cadaverous look, but I was still alive. I swiftly slipped into the engine cabin to get to the sleeping area to join my sisters. It seemed like every muscle of my body was used up. I could not even lift my hands and knees anymore. I passed out halfway into the engine room.

The next thing I know it was still very dark and I heard heavy footsteps running on deck, from the front of the boat and quickly approaching the cabin. It was Tu who then thudded to a landing on the lower deck behind the helm area. "*Thuc day het!*" he commanded. I was thinking "What now?" I got up as ordered and slowly crawled outside to see what was going on. As I got outside, I saw this huge granite boulder protruding right out of the water in the middle of the dark, gray sea. The strange part was that Tuan was aiming the boat straight at it, full-speed, like a kamikaze. In the meantime, Tu was making laps up and down the boat and appeared confused. I was thinking, "What are they doing? We're going to get killed." I grabbed the tiller handle and tried to steer the boat away from the rock, but Tuan's hand was on the handle so firmly it seem glued; I could not move it at all. With both of my hands on the wooden handle, one leg on deck and the other one pressing against Tuan's stiffened body to gain leverage, I grunted. Again, nothing moved. I then jerked back and forth, my hands slipped from the greasy handle, and I fell hard, my butt cheeks hitting the deck. I grimaced and rose up to try again. But it was too late. The collision sent me flying onto the top of the engine cabin. I rolled a couple of times before I came to a stop. The boat split right in the middle from the front to the rear as if it was a giant nut that had been cracked into two equal halves. Tu lost his balance and fell into the water. A crashing wave came and swiftly carried him away into the dark. I looked back and saw Tuan who was fighting to stay out of the water. He was sitting right at the edge where the boat had split and trying to balance himself with the movement of the half-floating boat as if he was riding a rodeo bull. My two sisters were in the worst place at the time. The platform where they were sleeping collapsed as the boat divided, and they both fell into the water immediately. They were floating due to the life vests they constantly had on. They raised their hands and shouted out for help. They wanted my help for sure because I was only about seven feet away from them. It was so strange to see that they were moving their lips, apparently shouting but I did not hear a word coming out of their mouths. I felt so helpless seeing them about to be crushed by the two bobbing halves of our boat. With my stomach down flat against the roof of the engine cabin, I tried to lift myself up to give them a hand, but I could not. I was stuck! One of the nails we used to hold our compass in place had hooked onto the fabric of my life vest. I could not free myself from it and the two halves of the boat were sinking fast. My body was already in the water. A crashing wave slapped me hard directly on the face, making me swallow a good-sized gulp of saltwater. I began to cough and choke under the water. I could not breathe. As a person experiencing near death, I fought with all the energy I had left to stay alive. With strings of bubbles coming out of my mouth, I began to kick my legs and twist my body violently to free myself from the nail. At last the cloth ripped and I immediately floated to the surface of the water, gasping for air. I do not know how long I struggled under the water, but when I surfaced, nothing was there. There were no signs of my brothers and sisters. There was not a single trace of the wreckage. There was no big boulder in the water. There was only me alone in the middle of the dark sea. However, the sea now was very calm, almost like the water on a river. One by one, raindrops came down, composing a musical tune that could only be heard out of this world. They struck the surface of the sea, forming huge bubbles which were slowly floating across my face, where I actually saw my own bewildered reflection.

Confused and scared looking around, I heard the sound of an

approaching motorized boat. I turned my head in that direction and saw a small, speedy boat, coming straight at me, with all my brothers and sisters onboard. They were shouting and yelling. I believed they were calling out my name, but again I could not hear a single word coming out of their mouths. I thought I had become deaf. I raised my arms as high as I could and kicked the water repeatedly. I wanted to jump out of the water like a dolphin to make myself more noticeable among the many small waves. At the same time, I was screaming my lungs out, however they did not seem to see me or hear my cry. Their boat was coming straight at me so fast that it was about to run me over, like that huge ocean liner that nearly killed us the night before.

Back home, there was a young man I knew who, just for the thrills, jumped into the river from the local bridge. I did it too. It was fun. Unfortunately one day a motor boat sailed over that lad while he was still under the water after a jump. As it turned out, that was the last jump he ever made. Three days later, people found his body stuck among the riverbank rushes two miles away. The boat's propeller had chopped up his face. After that deadly incident, my parents ordered me not to use the bridge as a diving board anymore. I always listened to my parents and this time I *really* listened to them since I did not want to die faceless.

DAY 5

The Family

With that scary thought of having my face chopped up by the propeller of the oncoming boat, I took a dive and hoped that I would go deep enough to avoid the guillotine. Unfortunately, with my life vest on, I stayed afloat as a duck that it could only bury its head down into the water with its tail pointing straight up toward the sky. While I tried to kick my legs frantically like a frog and move my arms wildly like a water bug so I could dive the motorized boat hovered over my head. My face had escaped the killer blades. Unfortunately, I could not get away from the propeller completely; it had scraped up one of my feet. It hurt so bad that I let out a long painful scream with strings of bubbles coming out of my mouth as I woke up — from a nightmare — to a new day, due to strident engine noise. The deafening noise came from our second engine, the one mounted on the outside of the boat that my brothers had fired up. I really experienced pain, since my right foot was touching the non-insulated exhaust pipe of the main engine. I immediately withdrew my foot from the sizzling metal as soon as I realized what was going on. My clothes were soaking wet like I'd just gotten out of the water and my face was densely beaded with sweat, but at least now I was a lot safer than I'd thought I was. Breathing in and out rapidly, I sat straight up and wiped the sweat with some dry blood off my forehead, thinking that the whole nightmare of the boat wreckage had seemed so real.

I did not forget to offer a grateful prayer to our Lord for a safe evening and greedily ask Him for another safe day. The very first thing I routinely and privately did when I opened my eyes in the morning was to say a prayer while sitting on bed. Due to our family's business, we could never get together as a family to pray in the morning. This time my personal prayer had an extra special meaning to it; it encompassed many thanks that I could not express in words, but I believed our Father in heaven knew exactly how grateful and appreciative I was at the moment. The night was chaotic at first, but sailing with the grace of God, we finally had a peaceful, safe evening.

The earsplitting noise of the spare motor did bring me back to reality. I truly thought its muffler-less noise could be heard miles away. Blares of the trumpet probably were no match. It could be a good attention getter out in the open space, since the weather was nice and the visibility was better than the past few days. I immediately noticed abnormal clunking and rattling noises that came from our main engine. I did not know much about engines, but I definitely knew what they were supposed to sound like and this one sounded as if it was running without any lubricating oil. Its exhaust pipe spat out a trail of black smoke. Long, incessant service could certainly have resulted in wear and tear but what happened was that the engine's moving parts, such as the valves and piston rings, were damaged due to overheating from the lack of coolant the night before. To prolong its service, my brothers operated it at the lowest possible speed but it still sounded like metal grinding against metal.

After we had recovered from the nearly catastrophic incident, the main motor lost its oil pressure and quit running. While I was asleep, my brothers took turns trying to crank it back to life, but they were unsuccessful. Tu, my inventive brother, proceeded with his last option, which was to open up the engine head's cover and fill it with the thickest motor oil he could find. It was probably grease or something. Nevertheless, the magic oil did the trick by slipping down the two valves and the single piston, and supposedly sealing the gaps, providing enough compression for the engine to start. Running at a low idling speed, the main engine did not provide much power; this was why both motors were now being used simultaneously. We were not supposed to use this second motor unless the main one failed completely, but my brothers propitiously decided to start it up to take advantages of good weather and a relatively calm sea.

About seven feet away from me, lying in awkward positions, and giving an intermittent toss and turn, were my sisters. My older sister

Ly, seventeen, was a very petite, dark-complexion girl with beautiful long black hair. Not only was she a particularly comely girl, she also had a wonderful personality. She wore a blouse and a pair of pants that had been made from the same white cotton fabric with prints of blue flowers. Our family, along with most other Vietnamese people, normally could not afford to own many clothes. If we did not wash our clothes daily, we would run out of clothes to wear in three days. That was one reason we could recognize somebody from a distance — based on the outfit a person had on. I thought Ly had changed her clothes, because the fabric's patterns were a little different than the ones I had seen a day or two before, but after I observed them closely I could see that she actually had worn these clothes for five straight days without changing them. None of us had changed our clothes since we had left home. The added patterns I saw were just from dirt, oil, sea salt, and a speckled growth of mold that had accumulated for the last five difficult days. It was uncharacteristic of her because her clothes, although inexpensive, were always clean and ironed.

This was a time when polyester material was widely and cheaply available. We found many new clothes in the markets, especially extra-large sizes. Word was that those clothes were tailored specifically for the people of the Soviet Union, but that the construction and materials did not meet their standard, so we the general public in Vietnam inherited the goods for decent prices. Unfortunately, we had to alter these clothes so they could fit; and the excess fabric normally could be sewn into small-sized clothes that could be worn by little children. It was seemingly cute since a little girl could dress like her mother and a little boy could look like his father. However, we all had to be very careful with this new polyester. Kids in the neighborhood were running around in what seemed at first to be shorts. A closer look showed that these were actually pants that had wrinkled, shrunk, and curled up to look like shorts. My sister Ly used to iron religiously after each wash so her polyester clothes could look decent.

Still wearing a life vest, Ly slept with an unwashed but peaceful face. Her bare hands and feet were wrinkled from the elements. I think that she had only been on our boat a few times, none on the open sea, before this journey. I was not in great shape personally, but so far, among us five siblings, Ly appeared to have gotten the worst from our dreadful situations. Like me, she had not been drinking or eating anything. Her already thin figure was really diminishing; the clothes she had on were a couple of sizes too large for her by now. Other than those few critical times when she was up to pray, asking the Lord, our Savior, for help, I had not seen her awake at all.

Tuan and Ly did have one thing in common: neither knew how to swim. Ly's never learning how to float on the water probably had something to do with me. When I was seven or eight years old, one late afternoon, our father took both of us to the river to teach us to swim. The two of us, with life vests on, were playing around twenty or thirty feet from the riverbank where our father was lathering his body with a bar of soap. Somehow Ly slipped off her vest while we were out there learning our moves. To save her life, she grabbed my neck and hopped on my back, which caused me to sink and swallow several gulps of brackish water. I thought I was going to die, so I shook my body violently in order to surface. I believe I pushed my sister away, as I speechlessly headed for the riverbank. Ly, on the other hand, was flapping her arms faster than a young bird testing its wings for the first time. While she was doing this, she let out the most frightened screams that I had ever heard in my life. As the bar of soap slipped off his hands, our father dove into the water toward my sister. Within seconds, he surfaced and had her securely in his hands. After that day, I never saw Ly again in the river.

Lying next to Ly was my little sister Hue. Most Vietnamese parents loved to use the names of beautiful flowers to name their daughters. My sisters were no different. We had an oldest sister, who had married and moved out of town, named Hoa, literally "flower." Ly could be translated as "green and yellow flower," and Hue as "lily." Compared with other girls the same age, twelve, Hue was small. She also had shorter hair than other girls her age. Actually, she had a haircut that looked almost like a boy's. She was a tomboy and always played boys' games with other boys in the neighborhood. Now she wore a navy-blue pair of shorts and a light-blue tank top. She hugged Ly tightly, gripping Ly's blouse as if she refused to let her sister out of her sight. She was the youngest in the family and rightfully received special treatment from everybody. She got away with things without getting disciplined, compared to me. In other words, she was spoiled for being the youngest.

Among my siblings, I think Hue was the closest to me. While my two older brothers were already working outside the family and Ly was turning into a young woman, to me, Hue was like a brother who I could hang out with. Together, we used to play hide-and-seek with neighbor kids at night. We had a legion of kids of the same age who could be divided up into two teams based on where we lived in the neighborhood. The area we played looked like a war zone and several neighbors made their displeasure known. As kids, we just did not care. The game was simple. We had to find everybody on the other team before we could switch roles. As time went on, we increased our area of play, which made our games longer and harder. There were a few times that my team spent hours looking for people without any luck, so, tired, my sister and I headed home to sleep without letting anybody know. While in bed, I always wondered whether those hiders were already in bed before me or whether they were actually still out there hiding. I never knew, because we kids never talked about it. I guess we always had some secrets we just did not want others to know. That was why there were times when my team was the first to hide that I just sneaked home to sleep. Two or three hours later, after some kids repeatedly banged on our front door asking for me, my father got up and told them that I was already in bed.

Farther up, I saw the body of my father who — almost for the whole night — had been floating around in the bilge water of the boat. Still wrapped in the blanket, he had been put back in the original location, on the righthand side of the boat with his head pointing toward the front. His stomach now appeared as big as that of a third-trimester pregnant woman. I suddenly felt a sense of sorrow as I looked at him. I remembered his poor body floating in bilge water along with hundreds of loose items. It was like he had been caught in the middle of a hurricane and everything that surrounded him had been crushed into pieces. As I was thinking that he certainly must be freezing in that wet, filthy blanket we had wrapped him with, I could not stop my tears from forming. Throughout his whole life, as a family man with a golden heart, he practiced nothing but good deeds.

One time an itinerant beggar with two small children came to our door asking for help, and my father told me to get some rice for her. In America, we meet panhandlers at convenience stores or on street corners but in Vietnam needy people went straight to people's homes with a cloth bag in their hands. Generous people normally put either money or food directly into their open bags. I returned with half a steel can of rice. The can was an old fourteen-ounce condensed milk container. The infirm woman was not satisfied with the amount and she proceeded with the story of her family being hungry and having nothing to eat for the last three days. It probably sounded familiar and at the same time preposterous. Most of us might have begun fiddling our invisible violins or giving a "take it or leave it" order to the woman. But my father did not care whether the woman was being deceitful or not. Without ruminating over it, he went in, got the whole rice jar, emptied whatever was left in it into her bag, said he wished there could be more, and sent her and two little ones away happy. It was not a lot, but it was all we had for our family for the next couple of days. However, my father would not lose sleep over what we would eat, what we would drink, or what we would wear the next day.

In the same situation, I personally knew a person who had done the opposite. As this "angel" of God asked for more like she usually did, this insidious person went back inside, turned the can upside down, put some rice on the bottom of the inverted can, now resembling a full can of rice, came back out, and emptied the whole, dissembling thing — now a lot less than the original amount — into the little one's bag. The chicanery was supposed to teach that pariah a lesson as I came to understand from the parsimonious person. My father would never do such a deceitful thing — not even to the lowest life of our society. He was poor but very magnanimous and graceful. Still, he never lavished money on his children. He never gave me money to buy toys when I asked him to, but he always shelled out change to some beggars on the streets. I assume that his rationale was that his kids were all sheltered, clothed, and fed; they would not need anything else. He could never afford to give me daily allowances like many other neighbor kids were getting, but he always made sure, every single time, that I had a couple of coins to put into the collection plate at church.

He never used profanity and never raised his voice at anyone. He sacrificed his sweat and blood to serve his loved ones, but never asked for anything in return. I could not remember when the last time was that he had had a full day of rest. I grew up knowing that he was the only one who would rather be hurt than for his loved ones to be hurt. He always strived to support his family while serving as a role model and a spiritual leader in the family. Watching him all those years, I still could not emulate his positive virtues fully. He was the paragon of parents whose place could never be surpassed. Even though he had lain down, I believed that he was not resting — neither physically nor spiritually.

Our father would not sue anyone or complain to anybody. He lived in a perfect amity with his neighbors and never had any kind of invective for them. Still, one time a family turned him in to the local authority, accusing him of killing their precious bull. They claimed that our father had fed their bull with poison and said there were many witnesses to the case. Our father was scared and shook-up, because his good character had been challenged. Why would he kill somebody's bull? In addition, he just did not have the money to replace somebody's expensive bull, if he had to pay.

While our father was working around his farm, this bull was nibbling on dry grass nearby. Good-heartedly my father threw out some yam vines — from which he had already harvested roots — to feed this wagon puller. The vines should have been harmless, because people can use their young shoots as vegetables. The animal appeared to be loving the vegetables, because he kept on eating; so, our father gave him a big pile to enjoy. A short time after the bull finished eating, he dropped dead right by our farm. Naturally, our father became the main suspect. There were no lawyers or judges in our village, only local officials who would decide right from wrong. Facing this panel of officials, our father gave his side of the story. Witnesses for both sides were called up. One set of witnesses recalled seeing our father feed the poor bull with "bad" stuffs however, nobody had seen our father actually fed the beast *poison*. There was no hard evidence — only speculation. The other set of witnesses provided the officials with information on what kind of a man our father was. Because of how he had lived among his neighbors, they believed he was innocent. Because of his character, it was implausible to think he would have killed the creature. After hearing witnesses from both sides, the officials wisely ruled the animal's death as being from natural causes.

Nobody could figure out why the bull had died, but many were able to purchase some beef the next day at the market. That beef made some people very happy, because we did not see the meat sold very often. Normally, the only times we would be able to find beefsteak at our local market were after a cow had been sick or one had been struck by lightning. Other than that, people would not slaughter these precious animals for food. Bulls, cows, and water buffaloes were very rare and expensive. People used them to pull heavy loads that no person could pull. They used them to pull plows for faming, to save farmers' backs. However, they did not require their owners to purchase food, as these hard-working beasts lived only on wild grasses.

As righteous as our father was it was unfortunate that we could not keep his body at a better place than what we children were offering him at the moment. He was still being subjected to the same elements as his children and we could do nothing to reverse that. Spiritually, I believed that he had been right there with us fighting fiercely the night before to keep his children alive. As a result, God had sent His angels down to keep our small fragile boat afloat and our insignificant lives were spared. It was not possible to fully explain our ability to overcome such dire adversity. Humans versus nature without any divine forces can only go so far. Bravery has its boundary. Knowledge has its limits. Luck can run out anytime. Tuan was not strong enough to empty out all the bilge water by himself. Tu could not discover the source of leak without what we called an "accident." I certainly was not fit mentally and physically to steer the boat safely during such stormy weather. Finally, I could never comprehend how my two faithful sisters remained so calm, to continuously pray during the whole ordeal when the Grim Reaper seemingly held a scythe up against their throats. Where two or three came together in the name of God, He would be there, and our prayers certainly had been answered by our Father in heaven. It was incumbent upon all of us to do our best. When extraordinary things happened to us, putting our faith in the hands of God was the right thing to do. We were raised in a family that way, and even though our parents were not there to rear us anymore, we were pertinacious in pulling together as a God-loving family to prevail at the end.

I slowly crawled out to the back outboard to join my brothers who had been taking turns steering the boat throughout the night. The ambient temperature was comfortable. The sunlight, along with its warmth, was drying up the dampness of our wooden boat. It also seemed to evaporate our tears and worries in the same way. The changing surroundings renewed our hope and made us once again aware of our new, transformed life. There was not a trace of wind in the air and our boat again just carried us through an easy roller-coaster ride. The sky had dumped all its water and cleared to a beautiful sunny day. This was the first time I had seen the greater light sending a warm hello to us since day one. Blinded by the light, I looked the other way, and the first thing that caught my eye was the multicolored arc embellishing a beautiful blue firmament. The iridescent arc appeared larger, brighter, and closer than all the ones that I had ever seen back home. Many times after long, hard rains that had destroyed people's homes and flooded people's houses, these godly, beautiful arcs appeared, and they always portended many days of beautiful weather, allowing people to recuperate from devastation.

Every rain season there were many rainstorms, giving most people of our village a difficult time. People with money always built their homes on higher ground than everybody else's. Their houses — normally built of cement and bricks — were securely roofed with corrugated sheet metal. Those homes were always okay. However, the majority of the homes in our village were built low, at the street level, using clay to make floors and walls, and with palm leaves as roofing. When strong winds occurred, walls just fell apart and many of those natural roofs just crumbled and blew away. Of course, those winds did not come by themselves; rains would follow and floods were imminent. They happened many times every year, a regular part of our lives. After each storm, people simply got some new clay, patching up floor and walls, and gathered some palm leaves to make a new roof. After devastation, life just went on again.

On the boat now we enjoyed the sunny weathers. Dry conditions allowed our wrinkled hands and feet to heal. Right above our heads the sky was mostly clear, except for some individual, standing-still patches of fluffy, white cotton glued onto a high blue canvas. Those clouds looked pretty and innocent, yet they quietly expanded and recharged for another storm. There were no birds flying in the expanse of the sky, but two long, white smoky trails staining the blue heavens gave me the sense that we were not entirely alone in this part of the world. We were not in the middle of nowhere; we were somewhere. Knowing exactly where would indicate how successful we were at this moment.

Tuan was saying something to me but I could not understand what he was talking about due to the still-loud motor noises. Without a word, I gazed at him and saw him pointing at something on the water to me. Tuan seemed to be smiling. I turned, looked at the water right next to our boat, and saw some sea creatures. These creatures turned out to be a school of needlefish. At first I did not see many of them, but when I stood straight up and made myself at ease with the surroundings, I saw more and more of them. I had eaten these fish before but I could never imagine that they could get this big. I had seen them as long as my arm but these could have been at least seven feet long. At this length, I thought they looked more like snakes than fish. Things seemed to be at least seven times bigger, longer, and stronger out in the open sea. Like the dolphins, the needlefish seemed to enjoy accompanying us on our journey. We must have had something that made those dolphins and needlefish swim next to our boat. Could we have been their next meal if our boat went under? Could the deafening noises of the two engines have interested them? Could it be the petite size of our boat — compared to huge ocean liners — that made them feel comfortable and friendly? Perhaps they just wanted a friend like we dearly needed one right now. Maybe they were God's messengers who were divinely sent to bring joy and comfort to us, the mourning and sorrowful ones. Maybe their presence signified more wonderful weathers ahead. The time we had enjoyed the company of those playful dolphins, the weather was very cooperative throughout the day. We looked forward to more accommodating conditions where we could sail smoothly, without any difficulty.

I poured a cupful of drinking water from a half-empty, five-gallon jug. We always had five of these water jugs for drinking on any fishing trip. For the past five days, we had only used half of a jug. I took a sip, gargled, and spat out into the sea. I took another sip, gargled some more, and then squirted the liquid out to the water. Last, I emptied the whole water cup into my right palm and started washing my face with it. That was a daily routine when I did my morning personal hygiene at home. Since we did not have running water back at home, I used a small cup when I brushed my teeth. After I had finished brushing, I used the same cup to get water from a water drum to wash my face. Most of the time, a towel was not available. I had to keep wiping my face with my bare hand until my face got dry. I was doing the same thing at this moment. After my face was free of water, I opened my eyes, looked up, and saw my two brothers. They were staring at me with their jaws wide open. Even though they were speechless, their facial expressions delivered a loud and clear message. Immediately, I realized what I had done wrong and I apologized repeatedly. When I misspoke or did something wrong — as others would have done to their own younger siblings — my brothers would spank me, yell at me, or give me an earful. This time they were beyond simple anger; their faces were all red and I thought there was smoke coming out of their ears. If looks could kill, I probably would have been dead by now. For a moment, I thought they were going to toss me into the water and feed me to the fish. Lucky for me, they were not as savage as they looked. They spared my life.

Sea travelers can live at sea for a long time as along as they have drinking water. As a rule of thumb, we could expect to survive about three hours without shelter, three days without water, and three weeks without food. That meant that the boat was our most important tool to stay alive and the next important thing was our drinking water. To last weeks or even months on the sea, we surely needed our boat and our supply of drinking water. I had unconsciously been wasting it in front of my overly worried brothers.

This was the first time I had really had a good look at my brothers since we'd left port. My oldest brother Tuan's physique recalled our mother's side. Twenty-three years of age, he had a small frame — about five foot four inches in height and 120-pounds. His rotund face resembled a full moon; in this he looked so much like our mother. Culturally, Vietnamese people love to have their sons look like their mothers and daughters resemble their fathers; that was supposed to have something to do with good fortune. When a son carried his mother's physical traits, he would receive great financial wealth, it was generally believed. The same wealth would come to the girl who looked like her father.

Of all our brothers and sisters, Tuan probably had the lightest skin complexion, which did not correspond to our social status. Wealthy people were stereotyped as having this characteristic, since these fortunate people usually ate well and rarely worked in the fields under a scorching sun. Ours was a working-class family and like similar families our skins were usually as dark, dry, and rough as those of alligators. Tuan was just different. Usually he had a neat typical haircut and even though he was a construction worker for a company operated by the state, after a day of hard work he would not look as dirty and tired as at this moment. After five days at sea, he had become a lot thinner than he had ever been. With baggy clothes, he might easily go airborne in a windy storm. His skin had weathered to a shiny dark color, with streaks of chalky, white scratches. His usually well-groomed hair was now all greasy and curled. I saw his cheekbones for the first time in my life and his sunken, bloodshot eyes had huge, dark circles. I knew what dark circles around the eyes from lack of sleep looked like, but the ones he had were anomalous. At first, I thought his face had been covered with black patches of engine oil. Still, this observation did not seem right, so I looked at them closer, and these spots turned out to be dark bruises that he had accumulated during the past few days when so many times he had fallen and bumped into various objects. A countless number of cuts crisscrossed his knees and elbows, resembling the red-crayon scrawls of a one-year old. Some of them were still glistering with blood.

Culturally, fathers had always been the decision makers in Vietnamese families. Oldest sons would be second in command. For that reason, acquaintances always addressed fathers by their oldest sons' names. In our case, neighbors called our father Mr. Tuan. When a father died or went away, responsibility as head of a household would naturally rest upon the oldest son, who had to take care of his mother and young siblings—financially and by acting fatherly. Tuan, who had always been a carefree individual, now had to assume that important role. As young as he was, I believe it was hard for him to accept that challenge, but he did his best. For the past five days he had acted so much like one of my parents. For our welfare, he kept giving us food and water. Even though we could not consume anything, though for many days, he still encouraged us to eat. He chose to stay up to take care of the boat while allowing the three of us to rest. Occasionally, while I was awake with my eyes closed, Tuan had come in and put one of his fingers over my nostrils to feel if I were still breathing.

Tu was antithetical to Tuan. Two years younger, with a thicker build, he was a bit shorter than him and his skin was dark in contrast to Tuan's. The big difference was that he had an elongated face, resembling our father. Standing side by side no one would have thought they were brothers. Putting all three of us together, though, someone might have guessed that we were brothers, because I looked a little bit like both. At this moment, Tu did not look much different than usual, except for a trace of the physical and mental exhaustion he had endured during the journey. He had been a man of fine mettle during the past few days. The only thing about Tu that looked different now from usual was his stringy, greasy, long hair that looked like Rastafarian dreadlocks. I knew that he had long hair, but he always kept it hidden under his cap. At home, he had to fold and tie his long hair up and put an oversized cap on, to prevent it from being seen in public, because where we lived the government made young men with long hair cut it. The only time I ever saw his long hair was when he stood in front of a mirror after a bath. The more strictly the government enforced this prohibition the more many young men went to extremes to maintain their hair length. Young men loved to have what others did not. It was a matter of pride. Officers at our village used to guard the river bridge — a main route if people wanted to go anywhere — and they observed all young men who passed. Any men with hair longer than "normal" would be subject to detention. Sometimes they actually had a barber on duty to cut people's hair right on the spot! Guys like my brother had to wear hats and ride their bicycles as fast as they could over the bridge, giving the officers no time for second-guessing. The good thing was that I never saw officers giving out tickets for speeding. Other than that, these guys had to leave town early in the morning and come home late at night to avoid the search. The officers once stopped my little sister Hue because they thought she was a boy. They told her to go home and tell her parents to take her to the barbershop to get a haircut. Their mistake was understandable since my little sister had short hair but it was still longer than that of most boys, plus she wore boys' things, my outgrown clothes. She told us about this during supper, and we all had a good laugh.

I always wore my bigger brothers' outgrown clothes until I could not fit in them anymore, then I passed them on to my little sister to wear. My father, a tailor, always found the most durable fabrics, that could last for years to make our clothes, which were subject to wear but not to tear. I always thought that the main reason for wearing my brothers' old clothes was because my parents could not afford to buy us new ones, but my father denied that and he called it "sibling love."

He once told me that by wearing my siblings' clothes I would be able to understand and love my brothers and sisters more. If this were true, I would love only my brothers because I did not wear any of my sisters' old clothes. Anyhow, we brothers and sisters indeed loved one another. As far as I knew, my father would not waste a thing in his life. If the clothes worn by my little sister were still good after she was done with them, they would likely end up on our neighbors' smaller kids. If not, those clothes would end their lives as cleaning rags for the family.

I looked at the compass and noticed that we were not sailing in the same direction as we had been the night before. We were now sailing at a bearing of sixty degrees northeast. My brothers had changed our bearing at dawn. According to our father's well-thought and researched calculations, we would see land within two days if we were correctly on course. That was a big "if." We had shut down the motor for two consecutive stormy nights and we did not know how far we had drifted then. We were hoping and praying that our father's plan would work to perfection. Again, having faith in God became a big part of our journey. God saw and knew it all and we did not. We could only faithfully maintain our prayer and trust in God, so His will would be done.

As of right now, we did not know how many more days we would be able to sail at sea, because we were short in supply of drinking water. Not that we were thirsty, but we needed fresh water to survive. Since we had left port, we had not used many of our supplies, due to bad weather. If the current beautiful weather held up for the next few days, we would be drinking and eating again. That certainly caused a concern about our water supply. In the meantime, this was not our main concern; the conditions of our boat engines were. Our main engine sputtered, with black smoke coming out, and could quit working any time. Our ear-piercing, alternative motor was doing fine at the moment, but it had only limited fuel, two five-gallon cans, that would probably last us — at the most — two or three days of continuous operation.

If both of our engines failed, our last option would be the use of a sail that my father had personally altered from an old, gray parachute. The triangular sail was about twenty feet in height and ten feet at the base. Sailing was new to us since it was not practical to use sails on rivers. Most of our rivers were small and curvy, and sailing them likely would be impossible. About three miles from our port there was a good-sized river named Cat Lai where we had tried out our sail one time. People on boats passing by gawked at us curiously. A typical big riverboat would have a combustion motor and a smaller one would have a couple sets of oars. They must have thought we looked ridiculous, since we could not move at all with the irregular winds. We had probably picked a wrong day to sail. We just had no idea. Anyhow, we kept getting stuck along the riverbank, even though the river had a wide area for us to roam. I believed the winds were actually pushing our boat rather than our sail. We cranked up the motor and moved the boat to the middle of the river, and then once again we were pushed to the bank. I heard somebody, probably my father, say at the time that sailing was as easy as flying a kite. I flew kites all the time and this was not the case. After all our test runs resulted in a fiasco, my father put the sail away somewhere in the boat and I had not seen it since. The only thing we had gotten out of the trial was learning how to set up the sail in case we needed it. We just did not have a clue about its capability, functionality, or theory. All we knew was that it was our last resource if both engines quit running. There should be always plenty of wind at sea. We probably did not know *where* we would be heading with the sail, but for sure we would be going somewhere with it, according to our father. He perhaps knew a little more about sailing than the rest of us but he was no longer with us. We just hoped we would not get to a point where we had to call on it for service.

The Cat Lai River was also a site where some two hundred people trying to flee the country had drowned a few years ago. An organized group which had a huge steel ship collected money from a whole bunch of wealthy people, mostly Chinese descendants, who wished to get out of Vietnam. This was at the time when the number of fleeing "boat people" was at its peak. These people brought their riches in the form of gold and precious stones. The safest place to keep these valuables was to have hidden pockets sewn securely in their clothes. After a whole bunch of these people got onboard, for some reasons the ship started to sink, and hundreds chaotically swam ashore. Those swimmers were just a fraction of the total people from the ship. People with small boats nearby saw the troubled ship and tried to row over to rescue the swimmers. Then a barrage from AK-47 rifles erupted, chasing all potential rescuers away, leaving struggling swimmers on their own. The river was wide, and only a small percentage made it to shore and lived. The rest vanished into its muddy bottom. Two or three days later, people who lived near the river saw many bodies floating on the water and some of them had been stripped of their clothes. Whether they were stripped aboard ship or on land and then tossed back into the water remained a mystery. An explanation remained hidden, as deep as the murky water they all died in. The gruesome incident involved so many human lives yet it never resulted in any investigations or prosecutions. It was like nothing had ever happened or as if those people had been asking for it. Even with all the money in the world, people still could not buy their freedom. These freedom-seekers had paid the ultimate price — their own lives. Surely they died in vain as the result of failed promises.

Back in our village, people built their houses along the rivers. The river were their backyards. Our father docked and secured our boat behind a house of a friend of our family — right next to a public port — since our house was several hundred yards away from the river. While tending our family's boat at the river, I made friends with many fishermen who came and went regularly. People fished when the tide of the rivers was low, because fish were more concentrated then. When there was a high tide, these people docked their fishing boats and rested at the public port. These boats also served as their places of residence since most of them did not own any home on land. They rested until low tide came. Then they went out to their ideal spots to cast their nets. They would take any fish they caught straight to the market, either selling directly to consumers or to other fish vendors. Money they made would allow them to buy necessities. That was their way of life — a simple one.

Nighttime came again. It turned out to be a clear night with a few visible twinkling heavenly bodies. For three years that our family had owned the boat, I slept on her almost every night to let people know that she was inhabited and guarded, so that she would not be vandalized or stolen. Most nights my father came to join me, but sometimes I slept alone. I remembered that my father had told stories of many years ago of sailors who navigated their ships, crossing many great seas, by studying the heavenly bodies. Those were some of the

Picture of the boat taken in 1983 by a local photographer sitting on another fishing boat in Phuoc Ly, Vietnam. This spot, behind a house of a family's friend, was where the boat stayed for three years before she began her exodus.

many bedtime stories my father had used to send me into beautiful dreams. Before I woke up, to noises from people who were going to the marketplace, my father had already gone home to tend our family business of making tofu. My parents began their work at three o'clock in the morning and had tofu to sell at the market before the roosters started to crow. Before sunrise, I got home, giving my father and siblings a hand a little bit, since my mother would already be at the market selling our fresh products. On the first and fifteenth of every month of the lunar calendar, many Buddhist worshippers fasted. As a result, we had to increase our output threefold to meet the demand then. On those particular days, our family had to get up a couple of hours early. I also got home earlier to help. However, I had to leave for school by the stroke of seven.

Grade schools were divided into three levels. The first level was composed of the first to fifth grades, the second from the sixth to the ninth, and the third from tenth to twelfth. My school only had the first and second levels. Older students had to ride bicycles across town to attend the third. As a ninth grader, I attended school from seven in the morning until noon. The first-level students then occupied the same room of the small school in the afternoon. Phuoc Ly School was situated on a hilltop in the center of the town. It took only about five to ten minutes for most students to walk there. Most of us boys stayed after school to play soccer in the schoolyard until the first-level students began their classes at one o'clock. Sometimes, girl students also stayed and watched us play. Their presence really increased our competitive and aggressive behavior. Three-pronged slippers were the most common footwear for us then, so we had to play soccer barefooted. It seemed like almost everyday one of us walked home with a missing toenail. On the average I would be limp home, bloody, once a month. However, for the love of the game, this did not deter us from playing.

After we arrived home from school, most of us tended our family businesses or went to work for someone else for the rest of the day. I started to work, helping my parents, as young as I could remember. There was no such thing called "illegal child labor" in this part of the country. It was all about putting food on the table as a family. Still, I was one of the fortunate children who could work at home and go to public school to learn how to read and write at the same time. Many kids of my age or younger were not allowed the opportunity to attend schools due to their family's financial difficulties. These kids were born in families where they had to worry about what they would eat, drink, and wear the next day, all of the time. There were no social services available. People, young and old, who did not work simply did not eat. People would keep working as long as their health permitted them to work. I had seen people work for a living, who were eighty or ninety years old. However, that was rare, because most people would have been dead when they were fifty or sixty.

When I was eight or nine years old, I began to ride my bike with older neighbors to a rubber plantation — which had been there since the days of the colonial French — to collect cooking fuel for the family. This occurred during the summer where school was out for three whole months. After packing our lunches and water we prepared to spend a full day — twelve hours — gathering rubber nuts and nutshells.

Together, we rode four miles to a huge rubber plantation, locked our bicycles to the rubber trees, and split up to find our rubber nuts and scattered, broken nutshells on the ground. Six broken hard shells — that looked like human ears — made up a whole nutshell that encased three nuts, which were each as big as a human toe. Whole nutshells stayed on the trees until they became dry by the warming of the greater light, then they cracked and scattered to the ground. For that reason, we always went there when the weathermen forecast a sunny day. All day, under the umbrellas of the rubber trees, we continuously heard the cracking and falling of their nutshells like the firecrackers of a New Year celebration.

For a full day of work, each of us probably would be able to collect from fifty to one hundred pounds of shells, which would provide two or three weeks of burning fuel for a regular household. Along with these, we would find from five to ten pounds of nuts that could be sold for a decent amount of money. I never saw any of that money, though, because my mother always sold them for me. People then processed these rubber nuts to make bar soap — something that I personally did not use for bathing, because it did not smell very good. As a matter of facts, users of this soap smelled like they had been sprayed with tree sap. People used this soap only because it was the cheapest on the market.

Our marketplace was very similar to a swap meet in America. People gathered twice daily; one started before sunrise and ended before noon and the second, smaller one assembled around four in the afternoon. This worked out perfectly because most people only prepared lunches and dinners. Some people probably had small snacks purchased from street vendors early in the morning to keep them going. Only a small percentage, those from some rich families, actually sat down and had meals in early mornings. My family was one of many that did not even know there was such a thing called breakfast. Before going to classes, I normally drank a glassful of soymilk, plentifully available from making tofu, and often went without food until I got home from school to have my first meal of the day. Soymilk with a little bit of sugar tasted okay. However, many times we ran out of sugar and plain soymilk did not taste very good. Occasionally, I might have some little snacks purchased from mobile vendors during our school recess. Electricity was not available; therefore, people did not own

refrigerators. Buying fresh food and preparing meals daily was necessary for every family.

During the night my brothers had lit the bucket with rags and oil
to make us more visible at sea. We hoped that the fire would prevent
us from being crushed by a big ship, like had almost happened a couple of nights before. The black smoke it produced probably bothered
us more than the ear-piercing noises coming from the two engines.
Luckily, after a whole day of loud noises hammering our ears, everything around us seemed to become a lot quieter. I no longer heard the
whispering of the winds, the talk of the waves, and the conversations
between my two brothers. I believe my tired body tuned out all noise
distractions so that I could get some undisturbed sleep. No ships were
in sight but the weather was very calm, which allowed all of us to have
the good rest we surely needed after many days of physical and mental abuse. My brothers kept taking turns steering the boat the whole
night. With both engines running simultaneously, they really took
advantage of the cooperative weather. It had been hard for us for the
previous four nights and we finally got a break this evening. The devils must have given up on us; they were not out there roughing up the
sea anymore. We were truly blessed by the loving God.

It was a few hours past midnight. While at the helm, Tuan started
to notice a faint source of light against the dark sea and the sky at a
far distance to his left. Because of the roundness of the earth and its
water surface, we did not directly see the light source; we only saw the
aureole that resulted from water in the air. It was not very bright, but
it was surely some sort of light, light that indicated people. This light
could have been coming from a ship, an oil-drilling platform, or even
a coastal city. Tu was awakened from his nap to chat with Tuan at the
helm to decide what to do. They exchanged words for a few minutes
and decided to change coordinates and steer the boat straight toward
the light in hopes of finding rescuers. We could not let any opportunity slip away.

For about three hours, we chased this light source but it did not
appear that we got any closer. We could not understand the logic
behind our failure. Our first guess was that the light source could be
a moving object — moving away from us. The second guess was that
we were sailing against a very strong current, that we were actually

standing still or even moving backward. Our third guess was that our little boat was not advancing due to mechanical problems. We then hoped that either our first or second guess was correct. If we had mechanical problems, we would be in a lot of trouble.

Then the greater light came up, and nothing was within sight, just us and the water. An hour or so after daybreak our hope had evaporated like morning dews. Again, a conference was called to discuss our next strategy. Our first option was to keep the same bearing, in the direction of the light source, and to cross our fingers. The second option was to go back to our original plan. At first I thought my brothers had flipped a coin or something, but in reality they had decided to go back to the original course. We had tried to reach the light source but for some reason we could not get there. Perhaps, the place was not meant to be found or there might not be such a place after all. We called it an "unidentified object." Now, we had to forget that hope while we continued searching for a safe haven according to plans.

DAY 6

Land Sightings

There were some sporadic morning showers and we felt okay seeing them, since they did not come with a storm like they normally had. Where we lived, we normally saw late afternoon showers and occasionally we were inundated with a big system that lasted several weeks. It made perfect sense in the tropical region. As the greater light heated up seawater, this created water vapors which escaped into the high sky. The temperature dropped as the greater light shined on other parts of the world, and then the water vapor — which seasonal winds sent over the earth — cooled, condensed to become water droplets, and fell down as rain. I looked up and watched the light rain fall as I imagined bringing myself together to experience heavenly serenity. I could feel every single raindrop that struck the surface of my face. I closed my eyes and allowed my mind to shut down, as if I was standing still under a jet of warm shower that penetrated and relaxed every nerve of my tired body. A few sweet raindrops were more than enough to satisfy my thirst, as I extended my tongue to taste them.

Tu was more concerned about our drinking water supply as he spread out a small plastic sheet to catch rainwater. The plastic sheet was as same one Tuan and he had been using as a raincoat. When the rain stopped, I believe he had collected about a cup or so of water. It was not much but he still poured his precious catch into a glass bottle and set it aside. I thought to myself that it would be the last water I would drink, because it looked very murky. However, we did not know what was going to happen to us. Perhaps that tiny amount of water would keep us alive for an extra day or two in the near future.

Right around noontime, Tuan was excited and yelled aloud that he had spotted land. His eyes brightened. His face was full of life. He jumped up and down while pointing his index finger straight ahead. Tu and I looked straight ahead to confirm his claim. We looked, looked, and looked again. Binoculars would have been helpful, but we did not have them onboard. Binoculars were considered military equipment. Civilians could not own one under the Communist rule at the time. I lowered my eyelids, trying to make out the gray matter that Tuan had pointed out. It took both of us a few minutes to focus our vision that far and then we sorrowfully concluded that what Tuan saw had actually been low-flying gray clouds at the distant horizon. They would probably turn black very soon and become another rainstorm that we would encounter. Knowing that his vision was tenuous, Tuan went along with us and agreed. He was so eager, jumping the gun, because his hope of spotting land had built up enormously. According to plans, we ought to have seen some kind of landmass after sailing this many days. His celebration was ruined. I knew that he was very disappointed to accept the fact that his vision had just been a result of a false hope. We all wanted to see land as much as he did, but we had to face reality and keep surging on against the unpredictable, potentially human-swallowing sea.

About three hours later, Tuan again shouted out in excitement, "*Dat kia!*" I thought to myself that he must have been hallucinating again. Tu grunted, getting out of the cabin and telling Tuan to take a break. However Tuan kept insisting that what he was seeing were not clouds but land. With a singing tone in Tuan's voice and a continuous stamping of his feet, I could feel his certainty this time. I dragged my feet right behind Tu to the back outboard. We both turned around and looked straight ahead. The greater light was so bright that it blinded my eyes right away, so I shied away for a few seconds. I then used my hands as a visor to shield my eyes, and looked straight ahead. Tu said that he could not see anything. Equipped with better vision than the two, I had to admit that I did not see any land. What we saw was a soft white background above the sea surface. There was no visible lands as Tuan had claimed.

Tu commented that Tuan was seeing things and said it was time for him to go inside to rest. I totally concurred with his assessment. To Tuan this felt like a slap in the face and he exploded in wrath. His

scurrilous language stunned Tu and me because we had never heard
him talk this way before, especially to his own brothers. He was always
a laconic, soft-spoken, and urbane individual. Our parents strictly
would not allow us to use bad words at all. They led by example and
we all had to live according to their well-behaved manner. For a few
seconds he screamed, probably letting out all his hidden frustration
that had built up inside of him for so many years. Tu and I just stood
there, absorbing strings of verbal abuse, speechless. After shouting all
those forbidden words, he either felt better or used up of his vocabu-
lary, and stopped. He then asked us without acrimony to focus and to
concentrate — just once. He calmly said that this was very important,
so we had to try a little bit harder. He was so positive, plus I was hopeful that there were lands ahead like he said, so I closed my eyes, cleared
my mind, took a couple of deep breath, opened my eyes, and zoomed
into the area right above the panoramic sea surface. To my astonishment, there *was*, like my brother had said, a faint, gray, zigzag outline — barely above the sea surface — against a slightly lighter
background of the sky. The gray outline was as thin as a light pencil
line on a piece of soft-white paper, but it was indeed different from
anything I had seen so far. It was distant and looked fuzzy, but I firmly
believed it was a stretch of land. I proclaimed my brother's discovery,
in jubilation. I victoriously raised my fist and enthusiastically confirmed
Tuan's claim to Tu. I do not know where I got my energy from, but I
jumped up and down laughing like a little kid whose school principal
had just came into his classroom to inform that class had been can-
celed for a whole day because the teacher was sick. Tu still could not
see what we saw, due to his poorer eyesight; therefore, he played Saint
Thomas and remained skeptical. However, when I positively
reconfirmed the appearance of land, he — even though still having
doubt in the back of his mind — joined us to rejoice the sightings. I
went inside to deliver the news to my sisters. But there was no need
for me to say anything, since they already heard our celebration and
were ecstatically repeatedly and thanking the good Lord.

A few hours later, the faintly colored thin line appeared higher
and darker above the sea surface. Now it was clear: this was unmistak-
ably land, and we felt a true sense of self-accomplishment. This also
was the first time I actually felt that we were on the verge of escaping
the wrath of the deep sea. Our main engine was not running well and

it certainly would fail soon; the spare motor would soon be running out of gasoline; and our boat structurally might not be able to withstand another stormy night. Rescue by ship had been crossed out as a likelihood. We were on our own. Reaching land was the ultimate goal for staying alive and at this moment we were within reach of safe haven.

The greater light already had now moved to other regions on the far side of the visible landmass, but there was still plenty of daylight for us to study the landscape. The strip of land in front of us looked like a long range of mountains, which appeared as a curvy silhouette against the lighter western sky. While we were still some tens of miles from achieving our goal, Tu ordered all of us to put our life vests back. There was no need for my sisters to do so, since they always had theirs on. As I was slipping on my vest, a helicopter suddenly appeared, almost right above our heads, flying in same direction as we were sailing. The white-with-blue-stripes copter came out of nowhere and whizzed hurriedly toward the land as if somebody was late for dinner. Its presence caught all of us off guard. It came and went faster than a Polaroid picture developed. By the time we had fully realized its existence it was completely gone from our sight. Nonetheless it was a welcoming sign because we knew we had come to a place with inhabitants; whether friend or foe was still waiting to be seen. Arriving at a place where nobody lived was crossed off our minds immediately. It also discredited all the unreliable information we had learned from books and movies about cannibals scattered throughout remote regions of the world, native people who captured foreign explorers, tied them up like hogs, and roasted them for suppers. We didn't think that cannibals flew helicopters, and my brothers slightly steered the boat to the left, trying to trail its path with the intention of arriving at the same place it was heading.

Then, everything became very dark against a gray sky. Noticeable things around us seemed to be disappearing fast, except for the gentle crashing of waves against our boat and the cool breeze against our bodies. A touch of the wind sent chills all over my body as if I were walking near a haunted house.

Back home our church was a few hundred yards away from the main road. To get to it we had to walk by an abandoned house that had the reputation of being the spookiest place in the village. There were many times that homeless people had tried to make it their living quarters, but every time they were gone within a few days, claiming that they had seen an apparition there. I never believed in ghosts but the talk of the town was embedded into my head and would not go away. I had no problem walking by the house during the day but, it became almost a forbidden place for me at night. On those particular Sundays when I served as an altar boy, I had to be at church by four o'clock to help our priest celebrating the early morning mass. I usually stopped at the main road and waited to walk with other churchgoers. Because it was an early mass, there were not that many people going. Sometimes nobody was there. I preferred taking a longer route — an extra ten minutes — to the church. Unfortunately, there were times when I was late and had to walk by this forbidden place by myself while repeating the Hail Mary aloud. I would walk as fast as I could and look straight ahead like a race horse with blinders on. That same eerie thought lingered in my mind at this very moment.

Suddenly, there were flames flickering on a shore. My brothers readjusted our direction, sailing toward the flames and using them as guiding lights. Questions began to pop up in our minds. Where could we be? Who were we going to meet? Were there any underwater boulders that our boat could run into? All critical questions pointed to one: what was going to happen to us next? All the physical parts of the journey became meaningless to us now. What would happen to us had become a mental game we had to endure. Our anxiety reached a new, higher level. Everything surrounding us appeared so scarily calm that there seemed to be something waiting to happen. It was like a calm period right before a big storm. It was so quiet that by standing next to my brothers, I could actually hear their speeded-up heartbeats. Their breathing was in total contrast. When they inhaled they held their breaths for a long time, as if they wanted to consume every molecule of oxygen in that volume of air before they exhaled. In the dark, my brothers' faces blanched; mine became blue. I understood that my two brothers, as leaders, felt a tremendous pressure. They naturally had a greater responsibility than me, the little one. It was like they were dismantling a landmine and hoping that the deadly explosive device would not detonate, killing them and everybody nearby.

My brothers had shut off the second motor. The main engine continued running on idle as it had been running all day. If Jesus had allowed me to walk on the water at this moment, I probably could have outpaced our boat. I could see the fear of the unknown registered on my brothers' faces and they acted like they did not want to go any further and expose our vulnerability. Not a single word was exchanged among the three of us while our boat inched closer to the flames. It was so ironic that during the whole voyage we really wanted to get to some land and jumped on it as fast as we could; now land was in front of our eyes and we were holding off getting to them. We did not want to die at sea yet we did not want to dock our boat. I was so confused.

Out of nowhere, Tuan suggested that we should drop our boat's anchor and wait until morning to dock. It sounded reasonable since we were close enough. The oncoming storms did not look too threatening. Our boat might be okay for one more night. In addition, this would lessen our chance of colliding with something we couldn't see. Tu hastily agreed, as if he had been processing the same information as his brother's. Tuan shifted the gear to neutral as Tu tossed the anchor into the dark, gray water. The anchor kept going and going until there was no more line left. I did not know how long the line was, but the result gave a sudden chill to all of us. It was indisputable sign that we had to continue. No conference was called this time, as Tu pulled up the metal stake and Tuan continued aiming our boat straight at the flames.

Our eyes were glued on those guiding lights and we were afraid they would disappear if we turned our heads. We finally came into an inlet that was about half a mile wide. As soon as we sailed inside this inlet, the water surface became as calm as that of a river. I suddenly felt only a little presence of the breeze left. The more noticeable air movement was our own breathing. We slowly approached our lighted destination as the inlet became narrower. Even though it was dark, it was close enough for us to see good-sized trees, large bushes, and giant granite rocks on both sides. The hills and mountains appeared very different than where we came from. In Vung Tau Province we mostly saw flat muddy or sandy seashores and marshes in coastal areas. Only northern Vietnam's seashores had this type of topography. At this point, the inlet was about two hundred yards wide; the walls on both sides were high and we started to hear clear echoes of our own sputtering engine.

As we approached our destination, the place looked huge and bright, in contrast to the flickering flames we saw hours ago. We did not see any livestock, wild animals, or humans other than ourselves. In addition, we did not see a single boat or ship in the vicinity. Out on the sea, we saw ships but no people. Now we saw neither. What was it about seeing some other human beings? Why was it so hard for us to meet someone? Our landing became even more mysterious. Cold sweat broke out at a faster pace. Tuan's knees kept tapping rapidly against the wall of the engine cabin. Tu continuously rubbed his palms against one another as if he was waiting for somebody to give him money. I can not remember what I did, but it must have been similar to what my brothers were doing.

We finally arrived at a sanctuary, a large concrete boat dock. This safe haven was as high as our boat, therefore Tu easily jumped on it, quickly tied the painter to a post, and immediately slipped right back onto our boat as if the place was sacred and he was not allowed to set foot on it. Seeing that the boat had been secured, Tuan turned off the engine. The cement dock had four tall light poles, each of which had three huge lights. The lights were so bright that the whole dock looked as if it was under full daylight. Farther up from the dock there was a huge, white, metal building with several smaller buildings attached as wings.

My brothers started debating whether we should go looking for someone or whether we should stay put and wait. They weighed their options very carefully before they decided to remain sit and wait for someone to initiate contact, since we had no clue where we were. We were very happy that we did not have to face drowning threats from the hungry sea anymore. We just hoped we had come to a good place. We were praying that we were not going to face any hostility for encroaching.

All five of us sat resting on top of our boat, waiting. We waited and waited. Then we waited some more, but nothing happened. Thoughts started to circulate in our minds that we probably were some-place we should not be. According to our plans, our coordinates, and the time, we should have reached Malaysia or Indonesia, two countries that currently had refugee camps operated by the United Nations. However, our boat had floated freely for two straight nights due to bad weather. Chances were that we had drifted northward during those two nights. We did not know. Looking at the surrounding land-scape, we thought that we might have landed somewhere in northern

Vietnam. At home, we heard eerie stories about boats that had arrived at an island called Con Dao where the Vietnamese government used to house hardcore prisoners. Some "boat people" got to this island and thought they had escaped the horrible Communist regime; instead they were arrested and thrown in jail for trying to flee the country.

As children of a military man from a former government, we were not allowed to attend college after grade school. We belonged in a group that was labeled "descendants of family with unclean records." According to the peremptory government, we were born in a family that had three strikes against us. One was that our family had run away from the Communists of the North in 1954, when the French left Vietnam and the country was divided into two. As residents of the North, my grandparents were smart enough to flee to the free country of the South. Unfortunately, after 1975, the North and South united, and they ran out of real estate to run to and were stuck with the Communists. The second strike was that our family was Christian. Communists did not believe in any gods. In fact, they were flat-out against any organized groups, since they saw in assembled groups the power to overthrow their rule. Moreover, the Communist government was very insecure. Its citizens were not granted the freedom of worship, speech, the press, and assembly. People had no right to bear arms. They had no protection from unreasonable search and seizure. They did not have the right to a speedy trial by their peers. They also did not have any protection from self-incrimination. In short, the citizens of Vietnam did not have one single "right" as stated in the Bill of Rights of the U.S. Constitution. The third strike against us was that our father had worked for the former South Vietnamese military. In the Communists' eyes, he was their enemy. Nevertheless, by the grace of God, we were allowed to live within our means, though we had no freedom at all. I guessed we had to be thankful for that.

My oldest sister, Hoa, went to a vocational school to become a nursing assistant and worked for a health clinic that served the workers of state-operated companies. Without a higher education, Tuan worked as a mason for a government-owned construction company. In 1979, Tu had dropped out of school before he finished the third level, due to our family's financial situation. As a seventeen-year-old, he smuggled firewood by bicycle into the city for a living. Whatever money he made he would take it home to supplement our family's income.

There were a few times that officers of the government — due to the ban of movement of fuel — confiscated his wood. Tu really struggled doing businesses in the big city, as one time he had lost his bicycle to some scam artist. He had to hitchhike to get home. Losing a bicycle was a big blow to our entire family, because we'd had to save for years before we'd been able to purchase one.

Tu was then subject to the military draft. At the time, the Vietnamese government needed conscripted soldiers to fight the civil war in Cambodia to remove the Khmer Rouge from power. This had a negative effect on the country's relationship with China, which launched a brief incursion into northern Vietnam that in turn required even more soldiers. The domino effect caused Vietnam to rely even more heavily on Soviet economic and military aid.

Quite a few young men from our village went out and never came back alive. In fact, their families did not even receive their remains for proper burial. Our father knew well the difficult lives of soldiers during wartime and would not allow his son to follow his footsteps. He paid some underground people money to take Tu out of the country by boat. This was the time when tens of thousands of people loaded onto small fishing boats and headed out to the South China Sea, hoping to be rescued by ships from various free nations. Tu was supposed to be one in a large group of escapees who were being transported by several small fishing boats to a bigger boat anchored nearby in the open sea to avoid searches of the river patrollers. Everything was done in secrecy because once information was leaked to the authorities, everybody could be arrested and everything, including the boats, could be confiscated. That big boat received supplies, such as fuel, food, and drinking water, from other smaller fishing boats, as planned. After all supplies were loaded and potential escapees were onboard, the big boat would begin the journey for freedom.

Unfortunately, word got out. The river patrollers raided the vessel and captured everybody onboard, including Tu. My brother was sent to jail for almost a year for that "crime," which was tantamount to treason. The jail conditions were unimaginable. It was so crowded that inmates only had a spot to sit in, with knees touching their cheeks. They were jammed together, side by side, at all times. Every day each individual would receive a couple liters of water and two small bowls of steamed rice. To Tu, it was like hell on earth. He would have preferred dying at sea rather than going back to jail. His unforgettable personal experience had weighed heavily when he had decided to keep on sailing rather than go back home after our father's accident. Children of wealthy families normally ended up staying in jail a lot longer than those of poorer families. Their rich parents had to spend all kinds of money to bail them out. Our family did not have that kind of money; therefore our father only went and visited Tu a few times, to bring him some food and medicine. At the same time he brought some cigarettes to make friends with the guards, so they would be easier on my brother.

Besides cigarettes the authorities could not get anything from our family, so they finally let Tu go. Once he returned home, I almost could not recognize him as my own brother. He was so pallid that I could clearly see blue veins all over his body, and his skin was covered with red rashes and glistening pus. His body odor lingered for weeks and he looked like a walking skeleton. This skeleton was not walking upright, either. He walked hunched over for several months due to his sedentary position in jail. His friends teased, calling him a monkey. His head had been shaved bald. Inmates always had their heads shaved to distinguish them from other people. In America one might mistake men with shaved heads for gang members. In Vietnam, people would see a bald-headed man and assume that he'd just gotten out of jail. Once home from jails, those ex-cons simply did not walk around in their neighborhoods. It was not something that people could be open about. However, in my brother's case, his shaved head could have been a blessing in jail. Since there was not enough water or soap, head lice could have thrived in long hair.

I had learned about head lice firsthand one summer. Instead of allowing me to hang out, potentially causing trouble, my parents sent me away to a Catholic monastery for two weeks. My brother Tuan had resided in this place for a couple of years before he got out. My parents just wanted me to try it, because deep inside they really wanted me to become a monk, who would bring pride and honor to his family. Tuan had failed; Tu was no hope; now it was my turn. Life was busy at the monastery. They did their prayers early in the morning, at noon, in the afternoon, before every meal, and before bedtime. Between those countless praying sessions, they worked in the fields, growing their own foods. From dawn to dusk these Jesus followers did two things: praying and working.

Being a first-time "visitor," I got a relatively easy job, which was to water and weed the gardens near the complex. Everybody had to work; even the monsignor was out there with a garden hoe. I befriended two young monks who were about the same age as I — twelve years old. I introduced a few games to them including cricket and cock fighting, and we played instead of working most of the time, like it was my summer vacation. Whenever we were hungry, we picked and ate the fruits right out of the trees. We had been warned not to do such a rascally thing; moreover, we could not blame it on a serpent. The monsignor punished us for this and other misbehavior.

At night we all shared a huge wooden bed that was built like a stage platform. While in the bed, each of us had our own mosquito net to prevent malaria. I could never get my needed hours of sleep before I had to get up again for a new day. I normally required at least eight hours of sleep a day, which I never received at this place. Life was hard for all young men who were following the footsteps of Jesus. The extreme conditions could easily explain why Tuan had left the place after two years. I would have left it after just one day if my house had been in walking distance. Those few young men who stuck around the monastery for years were truly men of God.

At the end of two weeks, I was glad to see my father come to take me home. On the bus ride home, my father did not say anything except to mention that I had been a bad influence on the two boys according to the monsignor. His unenthusiastic words made it evident that this would be the last time he would send me to this place. A few days after I got home, my mother suspected me having head lice since I kept scratching my head. She made me sit in front of a white sheet of paper and then proceeded to comb my hair with a regular comb. Little black critters came down and sounded like raindrops when they hit the paper. The white paper now looked like somebody had shaken ground black pepper onto it. The difference was that these black pepper flakes were actually crawling around. This was an extreme case of lice infestation, so my mother gave me a very short haircut such as I'd never had before. A shaved head would have done a better job, but she did not want me to look like an ex-con. Short hair and daily lice shampoo got rid of the pests and their eggs after two months. After that day, I always wore my hair spiky short like my father did and never again required combing after baths.

As we waited, we were concerned, thinking that we could have arrived at a place where outlaws were hanging out. We could be robbed, raped, or even killed without anybody ever knowing about it. This kind of thinking surely raised our anxiety a few notches. Besides a dock and a few contemporary buildings, this place seemed remote. At this moment, to us, this place was no more than an unattended lighthouse that had shown us the way out of dangerous waters. Who owned or ran this place remained a speck of sand in our eyes. We had escaped the wrath of the ever-hungry sea, and now we were facing another unknown. Chills ran through our spines, paralyzing every nerve. It was not a good feeling to sit and wait for something that we did not even know.

For a long time, we just sat still and waited for a sign. However, no revelation came to our way. A cool breeze gently caressed our tired faces as if it wanted to wash away our worries. It did not do a bad job of bringing us serenity as it softly rocked our boat. We might have been resting peacefully on a hammock that our mother used to send us into our sweet dreams. But we were not dreaming right now. Questions and anxieties lingered, as time ticked away. The longer the wait, the more uneasiness stirred among us. I thought that everything, including time itself, had come to stop. It started getting a little cold, and we gathered closer together to receive not only one another's warmth the comfort we dearly needed at the moment. My brothers still patiently wanted to sit and wait for someone to come rather than to go looking for help. It was like they thought that there were booby traps up there somewhere, and the thought of this was scaring them.

Besides thinking about all the possibilities, all the things that could happen to us, we were studying our surroundings to find clues regarding our whereabouts. But we did not see any signs. This location was certainly neither a residential nor a business area since nobody had been seen. Besides the lit boat dock, this whole area seemed a ghost town. The only visible thing that had some white writing on it was a small blue crane sitting at the far end of the dock. The letters were small but legible enough for us to make them out: "Made in U.S.A." I was only about two or three years old when the last American troops withdrew from Vietnam. I was not sure about my siblings, but in grade school I personally was taught that the United States was evil. The most important association in our lives was the Communist Party. We had to live, serve, and die for the party. Everything else, including God, our family, and our personal agenda, was insignificant. The whole country was in the process of recovering from the ill effects of the United States. Americans were imperialists who came to occupy our country and bring all kinds of problems to our people. They destroyed our villages and killed innocent women and children. They were the reason why we had broken homes — wives without husbands and children without fathers. Since my father had worked and fought side by side with them, he was tantamount to the evil Americans. As far as the teaching went, I ought to turn against my father, too. With the will of the people, the North and the South united to force out these occupiers. My history book had a photograph of a white American pilot whose plane had been shot down by the North Vietnamese over Hanoi. In the picture, the captured pilot had both of his hands on his head and he was guarded by a woman with an AK-47 rifle, a woman who only came up to the P.O.W.'s waist. That pretty much summed up what I had learned about the United States in schools.

People were not allowed to own anything associated with the United States. I remember that one time my father had to climb up to the rooftop of our house to slap some paint over an old piece of corrugated sheet metal that somehow had a portion of red and white stripes on it. I grew up in a brainwashed environment that attempted to make anything U.S.-related something of the past. We all knew that things that were made in the United States always looked good and lasted a long time, and most of the time they were expensive and extremely hard to find. We just could not find people around with merchandise made in the United States. People certainly did not go around wearing clothes with "U.S.A." written on them or with American flag logos. If they had, they would have been asking for a lot of trouble. Slowly U.S.A.-related stuff became either scarce or obsolete. However, that did not prevent people from desiring to own American things.

Three months before our journey, I went to attend the funeral of my grandfather whose home was close to my distant aunt's. This aunt had a couple of children who had been picked up by the Americans after the fall of Saigon and who currently resided in the United States. During the night, while at my grandfather's house, somebody rushed in and mentioned something about American-made toothpaste at her place. Out of curiosity and envy, a whole bunch of us scurried to her house and wanted to try this. The only toothpaste my parents could afford tasted so terrible that I normally used only salt to brush my

Funeral of the author's grandfather, three months before the escape. The three men, standing by the coffin, dressed in white terry-cloth mourning gowns, are (from left) Uncle Ban, the author's father, and Uncle Thong.

teeth. Salt did not taste great either but it was quite effective, preventing me from having cavities for many years. That was a miracle considering that I had never gone to a dentist in my entire life. At the time when my deciduous teeth started to fall out like autumn leaves separating from a tree, instead of going to a dentist or waiting for a bothersome tooth to fall off naturally, I was asked to tie a thread to my loose tooth and told that the other end of the thread would be tethered to a doorknob. On a count of three, somebody would slam the door and that would yank out my loose tooth. It was simple, yet quite effective. I have never needed a dentist my whole life.

At my aunt's home, I brushed my teeth with Colgate for the first time in my life. The heavenly taste from the toothpaste was so refreshing that I did not want to rinse it. I kept brushing my teeth for a long, long time and I forgot that I had brushed them three times already. Maybe I wanted to remove all the plaque that had accumulated on my teeth for so many years. I believe my gums were a little tender afterward, but it was all worth it. It took a while for a whole bunch of us to finish brushing since there were only a couple of Oral-B brushes available. I believe we emptied the whole tube. Seeing our affection for American toothpaste, my generous aunt then treated each of us with a couple of Hershey's Kisses and a strip of Doublemint. That night I was in heaven. I learned to blow bubbles. We got the treats of our lives and all of us loved them. One of my cousins wore a pair of Levi's and that was something I could only imagine in my dreams. We loitered in her guest-room to admire every single novelty that her children had sent her. We listened to beautiful music coming from a cassette boom box. The most sophisticated piece of electronics that normal citizens like my family would own would be a huge, antiquated AM radio with dials as big as a teacups and an antenna as long as a deep-sea fishing pole.

After all Americans had departed from Vietnam, almost everyone in the South, but especially the younger generation, missed a lot. Material things that were readily abundant in the United States caused envy for most people. They dropped their jaws and drooled when they saw the phrase "Made in U.S.A." on anything. Tuan was no different; his eyes brightened when he spotted the words. At his company and at others, almost all machinery and heavy equipment had "U.S.S.R." stamped on them.

Based on Tuan's observation at the dock now, he was almost certain that we were no longer in Vietnam. He kept drumming his chest as he proclaimed his tenable theory. We all wanted to believe him, since the simple phrase "Made in U.S.A." delivered us plenty of hope and comfort. We had set out to sea to find freedom, and "U.S.A." represented everything that we were searching for. To us, the United States had everything. The place was close to heaven on earth. Of course, at the time I was thinking materialistically. If people walked into a dark room, all they needed to do was to flip a switch and there would be light. If people's drinks were a little warm, they would add a couple of ice cubes to make them cold. If their food was a little cold, they would pop it into a microwave to make it taste just right. Where else on earth I would find such convenience? This sign relieved a lot of anxiety and made us feel that we were getting closer to our goal of being rescued by the right people.

I can't remember how long we stayed put, but it was approaching a new day by now. It felt like sitting still and waiting any longer might turn us into stones fairly soon. The tide had lowered our boat about four feet. Standing at a distance on the boat dock, one would not be able to see our boat anymore. Suddenly, something happened our way. However, it was not what we wanted to see. A great brown and black, short-haired creature came out of nowhere, and now stood on the dock barking at us furiously. The dog was the first land mammal we'd met after six difficult days at sea, and he did not offer any friendly gestures. His bark sounded the same as that of our family pet when she saw strangers at night. Further, it could not offer us any hint of where we were, unless we could have understood the language of dogs. Taking no chances of being bitten, we sat still on our boat while the four-legged beast barked louder and louder. He must have been a guard dog of the area since he discovered us, probably considered us intruders, and would not go away.

We had sat and waited for hours while the dog, just appeared, did not have any patience at all. After a short time his barks changed into a more panicky mode. With his paws scratching on the ground and his intermittent growls between his barks, he seemed to be more than ready to jump down onto our boat and viciously tear us apart. We were just sitting still and prayed that he would not do such a savage deed. Luckily, a man with a flashlight emerged from one of the buildings and rushed to the scene in a hurry. Perhaps he timed it perfectly; we had no idea what the dog was going to do to us. With some commands from the man, the dog quieted down and retreated behind him. This man was not particularly large. He wore a white shirt and a pair of black pants; he had a full head of black hair and a dark skin. At home, I saw our yellow skin turned darker as we worked all day on the fields. Other farmers also had dark skin due to the tropical sunlight, but they were not as dark as this man. I had seen this skin color a few times in my life when I was in contact with the sons and the daughters of African-American soldiers who left them behind after the Vietnam War. However, most of these half–Americans were my age and this man looked the same age as my father to me. I was almost certain that this man was not Vietnamese. He stood near the edge of the dock and gazed down in our direction. Although the dock was brightly lit, where we sat was quite dark. With five of us sitting on top of the boat dolefully looking at him, he proceeded to say something to us while swinging the flashlight across our young and confused faces. I frowned a bit and put my hands up to block the eye-blinding beam of light. Normally, I would complain if somebody pointed a flashlight at my face, but there was no hard feeling at the time. I was just glad that we had finally been found. But we could not understand what the foreigner was saying to us, so we were all still waiting.

"Viet Nam! Viet Nam! Viet Nam!" Tuan shouted extemporarily. The way he proclaimed it sounded so familiar. It reminded me that before each Communist Independence Day, village officials actually went door to door to make sure that everybody had a picture of Ho Chi Minh on their wall at home. The government issued an edict to that effect and expected all its citizens to comply with it. The picture had to be hung higher than anything else, including our Christian portraits or figurines if they happened to be hung on the same wall. Luckily, we had more than one wall available to accommodate both without compromising. Our father, a law-abiding citizen, obtained the largest picture of the former Communist leader that was available and hung it with the frame touching our highest ceiling. Officials coming by to check were really impressed with what he had done. Our father could rightfully call himself a model citizen.

On Independence Day, obsequious people were required to stop working for a few hours and go out into our main street with banners and flags for a histrionic march. Our father always made sure that we would fulfill our duties as citizens; therefore, our whole family first went to attend the rally at a makeshift stage, where a few party leaders got up, delivered a few diatribes against the Americans, and devoutly praised their big brother, the Soviet Union. All their prosaic tirades were almost identical, and they all seemed to be the same speeches from a year ago.

I remembered being out there with a small, paper, classroom-made red flag with a yellow star in the center, chanting, "*Viet Nam Muon Nam! Viet Nam Muon Nam!*" ("Viet Nam forever!") While chanting, we thrust our fists toward the sky in rhythm with drumbeats. My brothers were very good role models — my father had taught them well; they carried the largest banners and shouted the loudest during the march. We, along with several hundreds of villagers, did a few laps up and down the village's main street, lost our voices, and then quietly went home for the day. We put our banners and flags in a secured trunk until the following year's déjà vu. Somehow, moths and rust always destroyed those earthly treasures before we had a chance to use them again.

Even though none of us understood what the man said to us, he miraculously seemed to understand my brother's chant. It was probably something he had heard before. Without any further words, he showed us his palms and started moving his arms like he was doing push-ups in the air. His actions came to us in an epiphany; we all understood what he wanted us to do. It was fascinating; we were actually communicating without words. He then sprinted away with his four-legged friend following him into one of the smaller buildings. I was sitting there wondering what was going to happen to us. Besides the aggressive dog, the man appeared to be very pleasant, even though we did not know what was on his mind. We came in peace and peace was what we were hoping to get.

Not even a minute later, that man returned with two men running behind him. These two men physically looked like the previous one and I thought they were brothers. The first man ran a lot faster since he was dressed for outside — wearing shoes, pants, and a shirt — and the other two men were wearing pajamas and slippers. One man was older than the other; he was the last one to arrive at our location. They stopped at the very edge of the dock and said something in their language among themselves and one of them waved his hand, gesturing us to come up. He gently leaned over with his arm reaching out, offering us a hand. Our boat was much lower than the dock now, so he had to bend over and pulled us up one by one onto the dock, as we stood straight up, extending our arms. After six days on the water, I had sea legs from the constant rolling and pitching of the boat. I thought it would be good to stand on firm ground, but I was wrong. As soon as my bare feet touched the ground, my head started spinning and I felt that the concrete beneath my feet was moving, as if an earthquake was happening. I lost my balance and collapsed as soon as the lending hand let go of mine. Tu was right there to catch me before my body hit the ground. With my knees and hands on the ground, I looked up and saw that my two sisters — who had suffered such debility — were also on the ground and the other two men were trying to help them get back on their feet. We hobbled away from our boat with our beloved father still lying inside. For a moment, I could visualize that our father and our boat had fused together into a single heroic entity. With one of my hands gripping Tu's shoulder, I turned my head to have an appreciative, good-bye look at her, like she was a martyr who had risked her life to save mine. She seemed almost sentient to me at the time and I felt like it was the last time I would ever see her. She was like a tank that we had ridden on during a hard-fought battle toward an unthinkable Pyrrhic victory. We had one costly casualty and the rest of us were like wounded soldiers who limped away to find refuge.

We were led into the largest metal building of the area, which turned out to be a very clean and nearly emptied warehouse that had two basketball backboards, making the place look like a high school gymnasium. Along the walls, we saw a few piles of stacked boxes though we did not know what were in them. One man laid a large tarp near the middle of the floor and instructed us to sit down and rest. Another brought each of us a brand new blanket that was still wrapped in plastic. A few minutes later they gave us some crackers and hot cocoa to drink, something that I had heard about but never had a chance to taste before. The hot drink tasted so good and its aroma was imprinted on my memory forever. This was the first time in six days that my stomach did not reject sustenance. It was certainly a good thing not to waste such a heavenly drink.

Even though the hosts did not provide us with any luxuries, we were so blessed that we had been greeted with a welcoming hospitality. Such delightful care from these angels brought thankful tears and heart-felt appreciation from all of us. We had been robbed, beaten, and left for dead on the highway, and finally these strangers, acting like our neighbors, stopped and carried us to safe haven. From this moment, I began to understand how much a small, nominal bowl of food means to a hungry child and how important a clean, dry blanket is to a freezing homeless person. I began to completely understand why our father always stressed the importance of giving to our neighbors. What I didn't understand was why he always handed out largesse to the needy more than what he could afford. Our family was not a wealthy one; therefore, giving when we did not have enough ourselves never made sense to me. Our family meals may not have had meat, poultry, or seafood delicacies, and we may have had to eat sweet potatoes, cassava, or more vegetables instead of rice, but fortunately we never went hungry. I may have *felt* hungry a lot of times, but not like a barely clothed child living on the streets and going without food for three days, someone who was truly hungry. After six days at sea, we were hungry and cold. We were orphans; we were homeless; and we were impecunious. In a sense, we were no different than those homeless mendicants who came to our home asking for assistance. Our father had helped them with open arms, now his children started to receive the same good deeds, food and shelter which our father had handed out throughout his entire life. Our father had righteously sown his seeds and now his children seemingly reaped the rewards.

"*Chao cac chau!*" A sudden greeting came from one of the building entries. I looked toward that direction and saw a middle-aged man approached us with a grin. That brought a big smile to all of us, since somebody actually talked to us in our own language. He must have been another angel that God had sent us. His bedtime had surely been interrupted since he was wearing a pair of light-colored pajamas and a pair of dark slippers. After we finished with greetings, we learned that his first name was Tho. Vietnamese people always addressed each other by their first names. Teachers never called me by my last name, since half of the class would respond, though, as far as I knew, we were not related. Tho was about the same age as our father, so we respectfully called him Chu Tho (Uncle Tho). He had left Vietnam in April 1975 when the Communists of the North took over the South, it turned out. He had married a woman of Chinese descent so he decided to seek asylum, then stayed and worked in Singapore. He worked as a helicopter pilot who transported workers and supplies back and forth from an oil platform out in the sea to this supply station where we were sitting. He was the only pilot; therefore, the helicopter we saw earlier in the day was the one he flew. We had to admit that without him, we would not be at this location at this moment. We did not forget to thank him for the life-saving sign he inadvertently gave us, when he flew almost right over our boat. At the same time, we were wondering if the oil platform Chu Tho mentioned could have been the light source, which we had failed to reach all night. Nevertheless, that became irrelevant, since all chips had fallen into the right places.

Only one question remained for us: where on earth were we? Tuan awkwardly popped that question. Chu Tho laughed and apologized to us because he thought we knew. He then informed us that we had arrived in Indonesia, a country that was roughly one thousand miles from our home. My siblings and I could not believe that we had traveled that far in six days, especially with two consecutive nights with our engine off. While we were asleep, it seemed that there had been a great invisible hand that had moved our boat from location A to location B on our father's plans. We had achieved our goal — our father's goal. My brothers punctiliously explained the trip, while Chu Tho used a small wooden stick — like a round wooden clothespin — to systematically pinch the nerves on the soles of our feet. He claimed it was a remedy to palliate symptoms of headache and dizziness. We had never heard of such a thing in our lives, but we went along with him and let him work his magic. He spent about ten minutes on each of us and his therapy proved to work after all. My headache and dizziness slowly disappeared into thin air. No medicine was needed, as he claimed.

Chu Tho was emotionally moved when he learned that our father's body was still on the boat. He consoled us while making it clear that our father had not died in vain. Our father was the reason we safely reached the land of the free. While each of us took turns conversing with him, one by one we went to a nearby bathroom to wash. My clothes were in the worst shape of all; my dark green shorts and navy-blue shirt had turned black. After a nice Indonesian noticed their condition, he gave me a pair of cotton pajamas to wear. While standing in the washroom naked, I could not believe what I was witnessing in the mirror. My short hair was clumped together like a dirty wig. My two eyes had sunk deep into their sockets. Flesh on my chubby cheeks was replaced with high cheekbones. My mouth was badly chapped. My neck seemed to stretch out a little longer. Blades of my collarbones were clearly protruding underneath sallow skin. My ribs could be easily counted. My stomach was caved in. Beside grease and oil, my whole body was covered with red spots, itchy rashes. I was a skinny boy, but now I was all skin and bones. At first, I thought the emaciated person in the mirror was someone else, but I was pleased that it was myself— alive.

The white porcelain toilet did not look like any I had used at home. Instead of sitting on the toilet seat, I crouched with both of my feet on the seat of the toilet. It was a little high and I did not feel comfortable at all. However, that was how I knew to use our toilet back home. After I was done it was not much, but I needed to flush it anyway. I looked around to find a bucket so I could dump some water into the bowl to flush everything away, but there was no bucket around except for a drinking cup. I used that cup to get water from the faucet of the sink and pour it into the toilet, but it was not enough water, nothing went down. I put my brand new pajamas on, went out, and asked Chu Tho for assistance, embarrassed. I thought he would laugh at me, but he did not. He gladly went inside the washroom to show me how to depress the lever that opened the valve, letting water down to flush the bowl. I thought that was neat but at the same time I felt so primitive.

Chu Tho gave us a prepaid aerogram to write to our mother back in Vietnam. He promised to personally mail it for us. As the oldest of us five siblings, Tuan naturally would be the one who was going to write. He looked like he did not want to do it, but he did not have a choice. Tuan took a long time wondering how he was going to convey the sweet and sour news to our mother. We knew that back home she must have prayed for us continuously and waited for our news every minute. She would be thrilled to hear about us being safe, but how she was going to take the tragic news about our father? Tuan took a deep breath, exhaled, and began to scribble. He did not even need a minute before he folded up the aerogram, sealed it, and gave it to Chu Tho. At the time, I did not read what he had written on the aerogram, but it went like this: "Dear Mother, Dad has passed away. We are fine in Indonesia. Please pray for us. Your children." That was simply it — short and precise.

As it turned out, our mother did not receive this pithy letter for almost three months. It seemed like a long time for the delivery of a letter, but it was just a little longer than normal for international mail delivery to where we lived, at the time. Even domestic mail would take three or four weeks for delivery. There must have been a hold-up some-where along the route to have such slow delivery times. People said that the Communist government inspected all mails very carefully before they could be delivered. They would not tolerate anything that could bring harm to them. Not only mail, but transportation was also in disarrays and inconvenient. Maybe transportation also had something to do with the slow mail.

One time the government-owned construction company sent Tuan to work at the Tri An Project where they were constructing some kind of hydroelectric dam, not even half a country away. Life was very hard for him because of breaking rocks and moving earth, but the gift was small. On some holidays, with love, our father sent Tuan a letter with some of his hard-earned cash inside. He hoped this would ease some of the burden that Tuan had accumulated while he was away from home during the holidays. The general public used only cash; wirings, checks, and credit cards were not available. After three weeks, my brother did receive the letter, we learned, but it was minus the cash.

For almost three months, our distraught mother lived without hearing a word from us. Our boat was gone; we were gone; baleful village officials knew what was going on, but for the record, they kept knocking on her door questioning her about our whereabouts. Her answer was that she had no idea, and she was being truthful, as she did not know where we were at the time. Being a woman and living by herself, our mother really had a hard time getting by, day after day. To her, days just became longer and longer. During this worst time of her life, our oldest sister decided to come back home, wishing to lighten some of our mother's heavy load. After we were gone, she was the only close relative our mother had left. She could and would take our place to provide love and comfort to our dear mother.

After so many months without hearing from us, rumors started to circulate in the village that we had vanished at sea. This was not the first time our villagers had faced this type of story. A couple of years before, two whole related families got on a boat and set out to the sea to find freedom. They were never heard from again. Some people said that they had all died at the hands of the raging sea. Others thought that they had been arrested and thrown in jail, and that once they had gotten out of jail they had become homeless and moved. When people would try to escape as a whole family their unoccupied house would be confiscated by the authorities. If they happened to go back home, they would then not have a place to live.

Learning a valuable lesson from such families, our father did not want to take our whole family to sea and risk everything we had. In case we were captured and sent to jail, we still had a home that we would be able to go back to. For that reason, at least one member of our family had to stay behind to look after our house. Out of love for all of their children, our parents had decided to part temporarily so that we could set sail with this peace of mind. After we had reached the lands of the free, we would be soon resettling in another country; then our father would try to bring our mother over legally. Our whole family would be united again. That was the plan our parents had in mind. They had sacrificed so much in order for all of us to have a better life.

Although inundated by all kinds of rumors, our mother upheld her faith. She went to church every day and spent hours praying daily for our safe journey. She became quieter and withdrew from a lot of people; she was always in deep thought; her hands constantly were busy with the rosary beads. A couple of days after we left, she had stopped doing our family business because it took our whole family to do the job. Many villagers started getting up later in the morning after the business was stopped. As part of our seven-day-a-week business, we started up a diesel engine every day at three o'clock in the morning. Its loud noise could be heard miles away and many people used it to mark their beginning of a new day. Occasionally our family was late due to oversleeping; then a whole bunch of people were late for work, and our family would get the blame for their lateness.

Without working, our mother was soon running out of money, which was not much to begin with. She started to sell and live on valuable items collected over the years by our father. Our father was known as the junk collector of the family. His avocation was to collect and keep everything he could get his hands on. His often-criticized character proved to be dearly valuable to our mother when she was unable to produce an income. His collection turned into a treasure — our mother had assets which she'd never known she had before.

Finally her prayers were answered in the form of that aerogram. The local mail carrier, our family's friend, came to deliver the letter as soon as she had it in her possession. With the unopened letter in her hands, our mother uncontrollably broke down in tears. Those tears were tears of happiness and tears of thankfulness that she had finally heard from us. She regained her composure then, opened the letter, and began to read. Because of the financial crisis of her family when she was a girl, our mother had had to stop going to school during her fourth-grade year. I had read letters written by her in which I would not be able to spot a single period. I always had a hard time trying to figure out what she was trying to say. While staying at home, she had helped her mother tending silkworms, since her father unexpectedly died, leaving the family without an income. Raising silkworms to make silk remained her family business for many years.

As little education as she had received, she got the message clearly and quickly as a lightning strike upon opening the letter. She fainted and the mail carrier caught her in midair. The unthinkable news that our father had passed away struck our mother with the "storm" of her life, a terrible storm that robbed her of the love of her life. This news had to be harder to take than the agony of not knowing our whereabouts. That once-in-a-lifetime storm that hit her was seventy-times-seven larger and stronger than all the storms we had weathered at sea. I could only imagine how difficult it must have been for her to accept this tragic news after all those long, waiting, hopeful days.

That same night our mother assembled a clandestine group of close-knit friends and relatives to gather at our home to do a quick rosary for our father's soul. Citizens were not officially allowed to assemble; therefore, the praying session was very simple. The news was disseminated throughout the neighborhood; then town officials came to our bereaved mother and labeled our family as "traitorous." Families so labeled, like those having lost their citizenship status, would not be able to receive any benefits, if there were such things, from the government. To minimize conflicts with the local authorities, our mother kept her emotions inside and mourned discretely. It took almost a year before she could publicly offer prayers for our father's soul at the local church.

Besides receiving the worst news of her life from the letter, our mother did acknowledge some closure and feeling of comfort about her five children whose lives had been saved by the loving God who ruled over the deep sea. A big part of her life had been lost, but she still had us for love and comfort. No doubt in her mind, she knew that her children would be having a better life ahead. Our survival and rosy future assuaged her grief about losing our father. Although the escape was fraught with danger, we had been willing to take such risks to find freedom. Unfortunately, those risks turned out to be deadly for one. Our father — whose life had become our indemnity — seemingly and solely assumed all the greatest risk so that his children could live on.

DAY 7

The Final Resting

We had a few hours of sleep before two different Indonesian men came to take us to a nearby island where local authorities would be able to accommodate our arrival. Chu Tho had told us the night before that they were going to do that first thing in the morning. These two men came in acting very urgently, as if they wanted to transport us illegally. None of us had time to go to the washroom. We got up and immediately followed the men to the outside in a line like we were ducklings tailing their mother. The dock's lights were off, the greater light was not yet shining, and we were hastily making our way back to our boat. A slight breeze brushed my calves of my legs and sent all my bodily warmth through the opening around my neck, as some of the warm air gently touched my cold face before it dissipated. With both hands, I immediately tightened the blanket that was still wrapped around me.

Once we got to our boat, I was very surprised to see how low the tide was. The top of our boat now was at least seven feet from where I was standing. As I shied away from the chilly morning breeze, my brothers jumped down on our boat to retrieve some of our personal items. They noticed that she had been ransacked overnight. The noticeable missing items were the gasoline engine and the toolbox. My two brothers went inside the boat and saw our father's body still untouched. They quickly grabbed some items that included some of our family photos, two strings of rosary beads, and a sodden Vietnamese-English dictionary.

When Tu and Tuan got back outside the boat, the two men helped them tie it to a waiting tugboat, so that we could begin another sea trip, this time with assistance and a sure destination. The light blue tugboat was about twice the size of our boat, but it surely had a powerful engine. It's beautiful sound, so clearly slow and distinctive, indicated the great size of its flywheel. We all got on the tugboat and began our voyage with the two men as our cicerones. During this whole time, we saw no sight of Chu Tho, which made us believe that he'd already flown out to the oil platform. It was sad that we did not have a chance to say thanks and good-bye to the man whose presence had a profound effect on our survival.

Without us in it to empty out the bilge water, seawater had been slowly leaking into our boat and lowering her quite a bit. The tugboat gradually pulled our little but now ponderous boat out of the inlet. We went tortuously between buoyant markings to avoid underwater boulders. Some huge granite boulders protruded at least seven feet above the seawater surface. They looked like an ideal spot for sunbathing. Many other smaller rocks that stuck out of the water looked like those termite hills in Australian deserts. Their dark green-gray color would have blended in perfectly with the water at night. I was wondering what would have happened to us the night before had we run into one of these underwater rocks. Our boat could have shattered into millions of pieces. I could not imagine what devastating condition we all could have been in. The night before, we were so excited after seeing the lights, we just aimed straight at them like a moth plowing directly at a light source, and fortunately it was a really high tide. We may have passed over these rocks many times not knowing they even existed. Again, we were truly blessed by our loving God with good timing and a safe docking.

We went through a series of inlets and channels separating hundreds of small and large islands. Most of the islands had greenery and rocks, and none of them were flat. In fact, all of them looked mountainous. These verdant settings were where nature showed its aesthetic form without any human interference. The crystal-clear water, the gray rocks, the green trees, and the backdrop of the gray sky with some low-flying clouds set up a beautiful, ethereal terrain that I'd thought could be seen only in pictures. The two men did not talk and all of us kept everything to ourselves, creating a serene environment where human souls could be quietly in touch with their spiritual nature.

While sitting on the tugboat, gentle, cool breezes brushed my face, making me extremely relaxed and sleepy. However, with a whole new world opening up in front of me, I managed to stay awake the whole trip to savor every bit of the placid scenery.

To my surprise, there were not any boats or ships within my sight. I was wondering, "Where did everybody go?" Looking back at the night before, I was glad that we had not landed on one of these remote locations. Our Father in heaven certainly had delivered us to the right people, at the right location, and at the right time, considering there were more than 17,500 islands that belonged to the country of Indonesia. The night before, Chu Tho had mentioned that we were the second Vietnamese boat that had arrived at that station. That was surely a rarity. Now we were passing through all these uninhabited islands making us realize what a blessing we had received the night before. This whole trip took a few hours but it did not seem long at all. Even though nobody spoke a word during the trip, I was sure that we all shared the same peaceful frame of mind.

We arrived at a town called Terampa. It was on an island very different from other uninhabitable islands we had passed. It actually had a large area of flat lands, beneath the foot of a huge mountain, where people had built houses and businesses that made up a busy town, with a good-sized wooden boat dock. Terampa was small, yet the cleanest and most beautiful town that I had ever seen. People had built beautifully colorful houses, all different from one another. All these houses had a decorated front porch and a backyard. Our dull-looking house was no comparison, because beyond our front yard was the street and one of its two walls was actually the wall of our neighbor's adjacent, brick home. This wall had originally been made of wood. Over the years, termites got to them and my father removed the planks to expose our neighbor's. Then he never replaced our wall, due to our monetary shortages, and our neighbor's wall became ours as well.

Everything here was in walking distance; there was no need for automobiles. Only a few cars and a handful of trucks were all they had. Most adults probably owned bicycles and little kids perhaps pedaled around town with tricycles. Ferries, commercial boats and fishing boats arrived and departed from the port frequently. Even though it was an Indonesian town, its population included many of Chinese descent. That explained why the town was a business center, because wherever

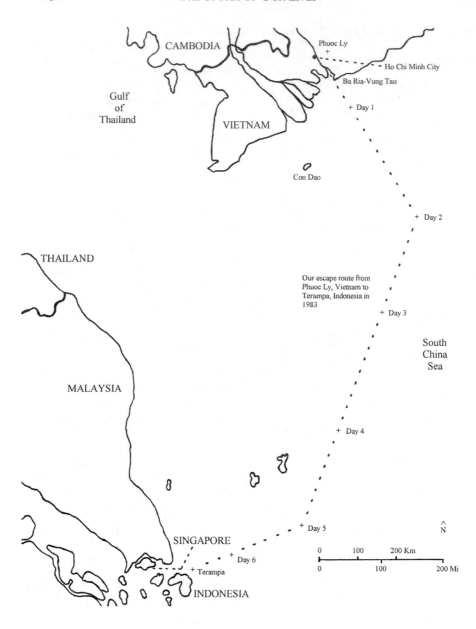

Map of Southeast Asia drawn by the author. The map (not to scale) shows the family's journey from the author's hometown, Phuoc Ly, Vietnam, to Terampa, Indonesia.

the Chinese lived they usually created a commercial town. Most people in Terampa owned and operated some kind of small retail or manufacturing shops. People from nearby and smaller islands came here to trade goods and services. Some operated commercial fishing vessels that brought in a lot of wealth. A small percentage of the locals lived up on the mountains' flat tops that were used for agriculture. The nutrient-rich earth, originating from volcanic activity provided local farmers with high-yield crops. I had seen a single banana that was longer than an adult's forearm. Each cassava was as big as a human leg. Green mustard plants were as large as trees; birds could actually come and perch on their branches. Crystal-clear water came right out of the rocks at the mountaintop to provide the locals with fresh water year-round. People lived very peacefully with each other. They ate mostly seafood and fresh organic vegetables and fruits. All these contributed to their salubrious conditions and beautiful appearance.

Once the tugboat was docked and our boat was secured, local officials came out to acknowledge our arrival. A great local crowd came out to watch us as we were still sitting on the deck of the tugboat. We remained passive, as we did not have a clue about what these people were going to do us. We were a little scared: not of harm's ways, but of the unknown. The number of onlookers increased, and as they filled all the empty spaces behind the safety rails of the dock, I felt intimidated and uncomfortable at being watched. This moment was a lot worse than the time I was in the middle of the sea and felt somebody was watching us. I curiously looked at this crowd and saw many of them covering their noses and mouths with the palms of their hands. Several of them were spitting on the water. I came to realize that my siblings and I had lost our sense of smell — and self-grooming. I looked at us from the crowd's perspective and I could not blame these people. We did look very filthy and were very smelly at the time. But there was another pertinent fact. Our father had been dead for seven days. He had accompanied us to safety and after seven days of tropical temperatures, his body had started to decay. His abdominal skin had probably broken, yielding a terrible smell as gases such as hydrogen sulfide, methane, ammonia, and sulfur dioxide that were released to the surrounding air. The pungent odor must have pervaded the whole, area. Word spread quickly among the locals, who rushed rampant through the seaport to have a glimpse at us and at our shoddy boat, which now looked very dilapidated as if it had gone through a hurricane.

Even though our father had passed away at the beginning of the trip, we had always felt his presence during our life-and-death ordeal at sea. Earthly, he was gone, but spiritually he was by our sides. He seemingly would not rest until his work had been done. That work was to bring us safely to the lands of the free. He completely prepared our journey and carefully planned our escape with an ultimate promise to take us out of Vietnam for our better future. He had put every piece of the plan together to work wonderfully for our benefit. Even in the worst situations, with the will of the merciful God, his plans saved us from the violence of the sea. At this moment, certainly his presence was felt, rippling across all the people who had come out to watch us. What they did not realize was that they were witnessing the living testimony of a true miracle.

For the previous two weeks, no fishermen had gone out to sea because the cataclysmic Typhoon Perry was circling the region. Its powerful rains and winds were so devastating that it was too dangerous to go deep-sea fishing. Sea traffic and other business slowed during this stormy weather. Everybody was sitting at home watching the everlasting rain that came down sideways at an incredible speed. During those few days, the violent wind and powerful, crashing waves had destroyed a large section of cement embankment along the waterfront. That kind of destruction had never happened before in the history of the town as far as people remembered.

Then the five of us showed up. We did not look anything like experienced sailors who had sailed on a sophisticated ship that could withstand the most severe storms. We looked like young and innocent kids who still rode bicycles to grade school. We came on an ignoble boat that most people would not want to use for sea travel, not to mention that we had sailed one thousand miles through a series of forceful storms without the aid of our father. The people here were amazed to see the five of us alive.

When we showed up a Vietnamese boat with twenty-nine people onboard had arrived at this town three weeks before. They were some of the lucky people who sailed the seas in perfect weather. At no time had they had to weather rough water and strong winds. I was told that their trip was almost like a vacation to them. After they arrived, many generous local people came and gave them clothes and food in addition to whatever the local government provided them. Some of these "boat people" were able to communicate with some Chinese locals in Cantonese. They had brought some gold jewelry which they sold to the local residents. They then were able to use the rupiah to buy some necessities.

Right after our family arrived, fish became amazingly cheap because the local people just stopped eating them. The "boat people" who came before us said that the fish now was selling at least half the normal price. Still, the local people were not buying them. Sometimes fish vendors saw us and out of pity, generosity, or for some other reason, gave us the fish for free. For a whole month before we were transferred to Pulau Galang Refugee Camp, we lived on free fish from those generous local fishermen and instant noodles from the local authority almost every single day.

The five surviving siblings: (from left) Tu, Hue, the author, Ly, and Tuan, standing on the hilltop in front of a Catholic church in Galang Refugee Camp, Indonesia in 1984. A small square-colored patch of cloth on their clothing signifies that they were in mourning. Beyond are rows of long barracks that housed the refugees.

We lived in Pulau Galang Refugee Camp for more than a year under the care of the United Nations High Commission for Refugees. We learned English taught by Indonesian professors five days a week. On weekends, we wandered along the beach to catch crabs and look for seashells. We were the sons and daughters of a former U.S. ally. During an interview, a representative of the United States was moved when he heard about our tragic escape and the loss of our beloved father. The five of us were promptly granted asylum to join our uncle in the United States, the greatest country in the world. At the time, most people wanted to resettle in America, therefore most refugees would apply to go there first. Refugees who were denied by the United States had no choice but to apply to go to other countries.

Bac Phuoc, one of the twenty-nine refugees who preceded us in Terampa, had previously worked and spoken English with the American officials in South Vietnam before 1975. He came out and helped us communicate with the local officials in English. The obvious first thing we had to do was to take care of our father's body. My brothers asked the local authorities for a burial plot and a coffin to bury our father in a small local cemetery. Bac Phuoc offered to help us to prepare our father's body for burial. But, the local authorities had decided to sink our boat with our father's body on it, untouched, out in the open sea. The main reason for this decision was that his body had already been badly decomposed. Authorities were afraid of the spread of disease if we handled the body improperly. Even though the decision had been offered with the most sincerity and sympathy, it was not at all in our best interest. My brothers surely were not pleased. They wanted to have our father buried on land, so some day we would be able to return to visit his grave. Bac Phuoc consoled us. He also explained to us that burying our father with the boat might at sea might not be a bad thing, according to the maritime tradition. Since our father was the owner, sailor, and captain of the boat, he would rightfully stay with his boat. In addition, we were newcomers, foreigners, and refugees who technically had no negotiating power over what the locals had already decided. They rightfully had the prerogative of deciding what could be done to us. Even with all the right reasons in the world, my brothers still felt very bad. Our father had done so much for us; and he had accompanied us for seven straight days. My brothers truly believed that he should be buried on land, out of love and respect. After hearing from all sides, my brothers had no further objections. Sadly they had to accept the only option, unwillingly. The decision was against our will, but none of us wanted to put up any fight to have our father buried on land. As a family unit, we had achieved our goal — our father's goal. It appeared that we did not have any more ammunition left to fight another battle. We had completely exhausted our energy, as if we had crossed the finish line of a long-distance footrace. It seemed like what could have been done had been done. We only wanted to give ourselves up to the Lord, our God.

Onboard a navy ship, the five of us stood restlessly on the stern and watched the ship slowly pull our little boat out to the sea one last time. Our boat appeared extremely sluggish; it had lowered a lot due to seawater that had leaked in since we arrived at the supply station. A few inches more and her lower deck would be underwater. Looking down to our boat, I remembered the red face I personally had painted on the bow. Within that red face, a set of black-and-white, angry-looking eyes always stared ahead sternly with determination. For a moment our little boat looked like a great big fish that had swallowed the six of us and only spat out five alive. She seemingly had let us go safely and kept our father as collateral. For six straight days she had suffered but had not broken. On this seventh day, this fish had exhaled her last breath and was about to rest in eternity. She would soon become the tomb and the coffin of our beloved father.

When we were very far from the islands, the ship's engine roared and its speed increased exponentially. Tuan was given an axe so that he could chop the rope lying over the gunwale. Our boat was under a lot of stress from the high speed. The stern began to sink; seawater gushed over the back outboard. Somebody gestured to my brother to quickly cut the rope. He raised his right arm but immediately allowed it to fall back down after Ly let out an emotional cry. His decision to cut the rope was wavering. For a moment, he froze. My brother shook his head and I could see that he was visualizing us at the end of the rope. Emotionally, he did not want to let either our boat and our father go just like that. He wanted to prolong the connection between our father and us, even though the longer we looked at the boat with our father inside, the more pain and suffering we had to endure. Again somebody behind us urged Tuan to cut the rope immediately. One more time he raised the axe high over his head. He closed his eyes and took a deep breath.

This time he was determined to strike that rope regardless of what was going to happen. He was so ready to make his move — and then the taut rope just snapped. We gasped. The axe hit the deck. The roar of the engine stopped. My two sisters wept and hugged each other. My two brothers looked on with stern faces. My heart skipped a beat or two, and I wanted to cry like my sisters, so sad over the loss of our beloved father, but strangely I could not shed any tears. This was the first time in my life that I did not and could not cry when I faced this much pain and suffering. My tingly and glistening eyes hurt so much, as if they were open wounds and somebody was rubbing salt into them. Still, not a single tear was coming out. It seemed that after seven days of facing constant death threats, I had turned into one of my older brothers, a strong-minded male of the family. Tuan immediately wanted us to start our prayers with the Lord's Prayer and three Hail Marys, and we all began the ritual with signs of the Cross. That was the simplest graveside service I had ever seen in my entire life. Our father had come into this earth as a simple man; he served the Lord fully; then he returned to the earth as the same simple man.

As soon as our boat broke free from the ship, she immediately spun 180 degrees; her stern now pointed our direction and she kept on sinking. As half of the stern had immersed under the water, the bow of the boat began to lift off from the water and aimed toward the sky like a missile that was about to be launched. The front deck faced our direction and that was the same area where we had placed our father. It seemed like our Father in heaven had positioned the boat so our father could take a final look at his children and at the same time his children could pay their last respects to him. Our father's boat, our father's tomb, and our father's coffin went down vertically within seconds, leaving behind a large pool of bubbles. Then the waters of the seven seas became a mausoleum. In seven days, God had brought our father a long way, to show him the free lands — the promised lands — his children would step on. However, our father was not able to set his own feet on them, regretfully. There was no question that his wish to provide a better life for his children was fulfilled. His mission to create a bright future for his children during his short life was accomplished. He was forty-seven.

Our father had given us our lives, the most beautiful things of all. He had carefully nurtured us with love since we had been newborns, and religiously raised us into children of God. Personally he had carefully studied, secretly planned, and avidly amalgamated every piece of our escape. He then gave us the most precious gift of all, the gift of himself. He had delivered us from Vietnam as he had promised. With the will of God, he without a doubt was by our sides, fighting diligently against the devils of the hungry sea. He had seen us safely step onto free lands — the lands that he had promised to take us to. His oracular utterances all became true, except for his part. He did not allow my brother to cut the rope to physically terminate the bond with him; he chose to go down into the abyss of the sea on his own terms. He was the captain of the boat who rightfully stayed with his vessel. Now he stays with her forever, as everyone else onboard escaped the wrath of the raging sea. Losing life in search of freedom was an exorbitant price to pay, but our father lost his life for his loved ones. His beneficence, love, and self-abnegation for us were so ineffable that there was nothing we could use to adequately repay him. Our whole family revered him because of his saintly life. We owed him our lives. We owed him our future. Our children owed him everything else. Deserving of high encomium, he is forever remembered in our hearts.

For all of our future generations living in a free society, with the grace of God, we keep saying thanks to him for the rest of our lives. Thank you, Dad.

Index

Numbers in *bold italics* indicate pages with photographs.